FROM DISGUST TO HUMANITY

INALIENABLE  RIGHTS SERIES

From Disgust to Humanity

SEXUAL ORIENTATION AND

CONSTITUTIONAL LAW

Martha C. Nussbaum

UNIVERSITY PRESS

2010

OXFORD
UNIVERSITY PRESS

Oxford University Press, Inc., publishes works that further
Oxford University's objective of excellence
in research, scholarship, and education.

Oxford   New York
Auckland   Cape Town   Dar es Salaam   Hong Kong   Karachi
Kuala Lumpur   Madrid   Melbourne   Mexico City   Nairobi
New Delhi   Shanghai   Taipei   Toronto

With offices in
Argentina   Austria   Brazil   Chile   Czech Republic   France   Greece
Guatemala   Hungary   Italy   Japan   Poland   Portugal   Singapore
South Korea   Switzerland   Thailand   Turkey   Ukraine   Vietnam

Copyright © 2010 by Oxford University Press

Published by Oxford University Press, Inc.
198 Madison Avenue, New York, New York 10016

www.oup.com

Oxford is a registered trademark of Oxford University Press

Library of Congress Cataloging-in-Publication Data
Nussbaum, Martha Craven, 1947–
From disgust to humanity : sexual orientation and constitutional law /
Martha Nussbaum.
p.   cm.—(Inalienable rights series)
Includes bibliographical references and index.
ISBN 978-0-19-530531-9
1. Gays—Legal status, laws, etc.—United States.   2. Homosexuality—Law
and legislation—United States.   3. Sex discrimination—Law and
legislation—United States.   4. Sodomy—United States.   I. Title.
KF4754.5.N87   2009
342.7308'7—dc22   2009042461

1 3 5 7 9 8 6 4 2

Printed in the United States of America
on acid-free paper

For Herbert Foster

Whoever degrades another degrades me,
And whatever is done or said returns at last to me...
I speak the pass-word primeval, I give the sign of democracy,
By God! I will accept nothing which all cannot have their
    counterpart of on the same terms....

For the great Idea, the idea of perfect and free individuals,
For that, the bard walks in advance, leader of leaders,
The attitude of him cheers up slaves and horrifies foreign despots...

Without extinction is Liberty, without retrograde is Equality,
They live in the feelings of...men and...women.

—WALT WHITMAN,

FROM SONG OF MYSELF AND BEYOND BLUE ONTARIO'S SHORES

Contents

CONTENTS

Acknowledgments

I AM EXTREMELY grateful to Geoffrey Stone for inviting me to write this book, for his encouragement as I formulated my proposal, and for his detailed comments on draft chapters. Among the many people who have given me helpful suggestions in the early stages of the book's development are Mary Anne Case, Elizabeth Emens, David Halperin, Andrew Koppelman, James Madigan, Cass Sunstein, and Kenji Yoshino. For helpful comments on earlier drafts, I am grateful to Mary Anne Case, Daniel Groll, Bernard Harcourt, Todd Henderson, Brian Leiter, James Madigan, Richard McAdams, Ariel Porat, Richard Posner, James Staihar, Lior Strahilevitz, Cass Sunstein, Madhavi Sunder, Helga Varden, David Weisbach. I'm especially grateful to Rosalind Dixon, David Halperin, Andrew Koppelman, Saul Levmore, and Jonathan Masur for reading or rereading the manuscript at a penultimate stage and giving me extensive written comments. But really, because I have written about this issue over a number of years, my debts are far more numerous. In particular I want to single out David Halperin, Richard Posner, the late Peter Cicchino, and the late John J. Winkler, all of whom formed my ideas on this topic in fundamental ways, both through their writings and through their generous conversation.

Preface: From Disgust to Humanity

"When I was in the eighth grade I realized what all the male fantasies that I had were about and that they were sticking and that I had to deal with them. I was terrified." That's what one gay man told social psychologist Ritch Savin-Williams, whose pathbreaking study of gay male adolescence contains dozens of similar stories.[1] The young man was terrified, of course, because he knew he was in for a difficult future in American society. To some extent, too, he had internalized society's attitudes: a student at an evangelical school, he had learned to feel horror and disgust at the behavior he desired and to think of it as base or animalistic, not suited to the full dignity of a human being. Many other gay youths interviewed by Savin-Williams felt fine about their feelings—and yet they, too, knew that they had a difficult road ahead, since many people, if not they themselves, would regard their desires and acts with disgust. "I knew that this was...the path that I wanted," writes another young man about his early sexual experiences with other male teens, "and I knew that I was on it. I knew that others could sort of experience what I was and I knew that other people would think of it as being disgusting."[2]

This book, although concerned with abstract issues of constitutional law, is essentially about the divide that teen saw before him: between people who can "sort of experience" what a gay teenager feels and people who simply think of those desires, and, no doubt, the teenagers themselves, "as being disgusting." For a long time, our society, like many others, has confronted same-sex orientations and acts with a politics of disgust, as many people react to the uncomfortable presence of gays and lesbians with a deep aversion akin to that inspired by bodily wastes, slimy insects, and spoiled food—and then cite that very reaction to justify a range of legal restrictions, from sodomy laws to bans on same-sex marriage. Partisans of the politics of disgust can barely stand to think about what that gay teenager did with his friends; they say, "that stuff makes me want to throw up," and turn away from the reality of gay life as from a loathsome contaminant to the body politic. Even to look closely at what that gay teen does is to be defiled. To be looked at by a gay man is probably worse, for it means being penetrated by the defiler. Although this political approach has lost ground in recent years, it continues to influence the ways in which many people think.

Disgust, so described, seems pretty nasty, a fundamental refusal of another person's full humanity. One might therefore think it a bad basis for lawmaking in a democratic society. Disgust, however, has had some highly respectable and influential defenders in the law. In Britain in the 1950s, Lord Patrick Devlin argued that the disgust of the average member of society was a sufficient reason to make a practice illegal, even if it caused no harm to nonconsenting third parties. He applied his conclusion directly to the Wolfenden Commission's proposal to decriminalize consensual same-sex sexual acts, which he strongly opposed. He argued that society would decay from within if it did not make law in response to the feelings of disgust with which average people (he claimed) view same-sex practices. More recently, in the United States, Leon Kass, until recently the head of President Bush's President's Council on Bioethics, argues that repugnance has an inherent "wisdom": it is a device implanted in our natures that steers us away from destructive and terrible choices. Like Devlin, Kass concludes that disgust is a sufficient reason to ban a practice that causes no harm to nonconsenting parties.[3]

Nor are these positions merely academic: they are in tune with widespread social forces. Today, large segments of the Christian Right openly practice a politics based upon disgust. Depicting the sexual practices of lesbians and, especially, of gay men as vile and revolting, they suggest that such practices contaminate and defile society, producing decay and degeneration. Like Kass and Devlin, they believe that disgust is a reliable guide to lawmaking. Although the influence of such appeals peaked, perhaps, in the 1980s and 1990s, and has since been declining, the politics of disgust continues to exercise influence, often in more subtle and unstated ways. We need, then, to understand why it is not a good approach to politics and law in a democratic society.

The politics of disgust is profoundly at odds with the abstract idea of a society based on the equality of all citizens, in which all have a right to the equal protection of the laws. It says that the mere fact that you happen to make me want to vomit is reason enough for me to treat you as a social pariah, denying you some of your most basic entitlements as a citizen. As we shall see, even the U. S. Supreme Court has held that legal deference to this sort of "animus" violates the idea of the equal protection of the laws in its most basic and general form. It also violates a fundamental paradigm of political rationality: laws made in response to such animus lack a rational basis.

Despite these legal setbacks in recent years, the politics of disgust is alive and well in America today, as many groups aggressively depict same-sex practices in such a way as to arouse disgust and then draw on that reaction when campaigning against the legalization of same-sex marriage, or nondiscrimination laws. Such appeals are often seen as not politically correct today, so other arguments are increasingly put forward. Disgust, however, has not gone away, it has gone underground. We still need to understand its force, and why arguments based upon it are bad political arguments. A closer study of the emotion of disgust and the ways in which it has been used politically through history will suggest some powerful arguments against disgust's apostles in theory and in practice, by showing how that emotion expresses a universal human discomfort with bodily reality, but then uses that discomfort to target and subordinate vulnerable minorities.[4]

Disgust has two opponents today, each increasingly powerful in social, political, and even legal life: respect and sympathy. The idea of equal respect for persons, surely a key concept throughout the history of the American democracy, combined with a high evaluation of personal liberty, suggests to many citizens that even when they don't think well of someone's intimate personal choices, they should give them space to make them, so long as they do not violate other people's rights. Such a politics of equal respect/equal liberty has long been the norm in the area of religion, where we are used to the idea that we should live on terms of respect with people whose choices we think bad, or even sinful, and to the related idea that such deeply meaningful personal choices require the protection, for all, of a sphere of personal freedom. The object of respect is the person, not the person's actions; but respecting one's fellow citizens as equals, a long tradition holds, requires seeing them as choosers and seekers who need a wide area of liberty around them, whether they use that liberty well or poorly (so long as they do not trample on the rights of others). Many people see sexual orientation as similar: a characteristic intimately connected with a person's search for a meaningful life, and therefore something whose abridgment or legal restriction inflicts profound psychic damage. Equal respect for citizens, many believe, precludes the infliction of such damage on those who simply seek to act on their desires without violating the rights of others.

A politics of equal respect is also by now the norm in the areas of gender, race, and disability, where we have gradually come to see that deep-seated characteristics are not a legitimate basis for the systematic legal subordination of a group. Many people now feel that sexual orientation is in important ways like these other areas. Like race and gender, sexual orientation is a deep-seated characteristic that has profound meaning for people, affecting their possibilities for self-expression and happiness; it should not be turned into a systematic source of social inequality. Equal respect for citizens, many now hold, requires not converting a person's sexual orientation into a reason for denying them a wide range of political entitlements on a basis of equality with others—any more than a person's race, or gender, or disability would be such a reason.

The politics of equal respect, in our constitutional tradition, goes hand in hand with the idea that the fundamental bearer of entitlements is the person, not the group, and with the related idea that respect for persons involves protecting certain spheres of liberty around them, in which they can make choices crucial to their lives. Articulating and protecting these spheres of personal liberty has been a crucial task of our tradition of constitutional law. This sort of constitutional politics is anticollectivist: it says that the interests of the majority cannot trump such basic entitlements of the individual, except in very unusual circumstances, usually where harm to others, or some grave danger for the whole nation, is in the offing. Such a political stance is not that of the left as opposed to the right; it is that of classical liberalism, as contrasted both with the collectivism of the left and the collectivism of the right. We shall later explore this contrast, as it works itself out in the area of sexual politics.

That "terrified" gay teenager needs, and deserves, equal respect, and a sphere of liberty equal to that enjoyed by others. Before he is likely to get these things, however, something else also has to be present in our world: the capacity to imagine his experience and that of other gay and lesbian citizens. Disgust relies on moral obtuseness. It is possible to view another human being as a slimy slug or a piece of revolting trash only if one has never made a serious good-faith attempt to see the world through that person's eyes or to experience that person's feelings. Disgust imputes to the other a subhuman nature. How, by contrast, do we ever become able to see one another as human? Only through the exercise of imagination. Humanity does not automatically reveal itself to strangers. No placard hung on the front of a fellow citizen announces that this one is a full-fledged human being (and not a vile bug or a piece of refuse). Seeing the shape of a human being before us, we always have choices to make: will we impute full equal humanity to that shape, or something less? Only by imagining how the world looks through that person's eyes does one get to the point of seeing the other person as a someone and not a something. (Sadly, racial minorities have long been seen as somethings rather than someones, and women are all too frequently so seen today, given the ever-present phenomenon of sexual "objectification," in which a person is treated as a mere thing.[5]) That crucial imaginative engagement has been sadly and sorely lacking in majority dealings with lesbian and gay lives.

Today, a number of social factors have begun to alter that situation. Central among them is the coming out of so many gay men and lesbians, each of them a child of two parents and a friend and fellow-worker of many, each with a personal narrative, an individual name, and eyes into which people have been accustomed to look with the belief that they see humanity in there. When the person then comes out as lesbian or gay, it is usually difficult to withdraw those ascriptions of humanity in favor of the old disgust-laden picture. Even the most shocked and judgmental of parents rarely get to the point of thinking of their child as merely a slimy slug. Most are a lot more generous than that, and this generosity influences their view of other gays and lesbians.

Together with this development is the growing presence of gay men and lesbians in politics, in the arts, in sports, in the academy, and in other places to which people are accustomed to look for role models—and, perhaps even more important, the growing presence of lesbian and gay characters in mainstream media, where countless viewers learn to identify with their stories and their emotions. *Will and Grace* is not sociology, but it has had a much greater social influence than all the sociological treatises on this topic combined, because it gets straight people to identify with the emotions of Will, as he searches for love, to laugh at Jack's vanity and frivolity in a way that is participatory and accepting rather than harsh, and to feel how a straight person, Grace, owes her emotional stability to Will's generous concern. (Thus straight people are reminded that gays are not pathetic victims, but creative moral and social agents.)

All of these developments have begun to produce what I shall call the *politics of humanity*, a political attitude that combines respect with curiosity and imaginative attunement. (The word "humanity" was used in much this sense by Adam Smith in the eighteenth century to describe the capacity for generous and flexible engagement with the sufferings and hopes of other people. (It is, however, much older, going back at least to the Roman philosopher and statesman Cicero, who used the Latin term *humanitas* to designate a kind of responsiveness to others that prominently included the ability to imagine their experiences.)[6]

The politics of humanity, as I shall use the term, includes respect. But respect, as usually conceived, is not sufficient for it: something else, something closer to love, must also be involved.

First of all, we are unlikely to achieve full respect for one another unless we can do something else first—see the other as a center of perception, emotion, and reason, rather than an inert object. Put that way, it might appear that this imaginative and emotional attitude is a mere instrument to a respect that might be arrived at by some other route. However, respect without this attitude is certainly not a complete basis for political action in a diverse society: for only imagination animates the cold and abstract categories of morality and law, turning them into ways we can live together. So, respect is politically incomplete without imagination.

One may, however, make a stronger claim, and I shall defend this claim: the capacity for imaginative and emotional participation in the lives of others is an essential ingredient of any respect worthy the name. Only this capacity makes real an ability that is a key part of respect, the ability to see the other as an end, not as a mere means. The politics of humanity includes, then, both respect and imagination, and imagination understood as an ingredient essential to respect itself.

We are living in an era of transition between two very different types of politics in the area of sexual orientation. The politics of disgust, which so long has called the tune, is facing unprecedented challenges from the politics of humanity, as the life stories of so many lesbians and gay men have engaged people's imaginations, as people increasingly see their struggles for respect, inclusion, and even marriage with the sort of sympathy with which they might participate in the struggles of a child or friend or relation or coworker—and of course most of us have gay or lesbian children or friends or relations or coworkers. The politics of disgust, however, keeps pushing back, and the outcome, where law is concerned, remains unclear. Even when we suppose that we have put disgust behind us, we may be taken by surprise, as people confront issues concerning HIV/AIDS, or gay bathhouses, or sex in public places.

This book will explore all these issues, showing what a politics of disgust has been like and why it is unworthy of America, and mapping the contours of a politics of humanity. Its focus is constitutional law, but its argument has implications for the way in which we see many related questions. Beginning with the well-known constitutional cases involving sodomy laws and nondiscrimination laws, I shall then move on to the contested issue of same-sex marriage, trying to sort through the legal issues and the related social arguments. Finally, I shall ask what a right of intimate association requires in the areas of "public" sex, sex clubs and bathhouses, and condomless sex in the presence of a risk of HIV transmission, arguing that in such areas the impulse to react with disgust remains extremely powerful, and disruptively so, as a determinant of both social norms and lawmaking.

The transformation from a politics of disgust to a politics of humanity involves almost every aspect of American society. Ideas about family, about employment, about the common good, all these are implicated in the concept of a politics of humanity, and this politics must be enacted and reenacted in each of these areas, in each region of the country, each time a new issue comes along. Like the process of gay coming out, which is often said to be endless, in that new people may always come along who have not been told about one's orientation, so too the process of transforming social attitudes is multifaceted and requires a new effort every time a new issue or group needs to be confronted and persuaded. Ultimately, the process involves transformation at the level of the human heart, and that means that it requires great patience. Nonetheless, these broad and deep social transformations are currently under way, though with an uncertain future.

The transformation I recommend will also involve changes in many domains of the law. Family law, antidiscrimination law, labor law, all are currently undergoing a complex set of challenges and reexaminations, most of which can barely be alluded to in a book that forms part of a series dedicated to issues in constitutional law.

Why, though, should one suppose that constitutional law has any significant role to play in the transformation? That domain of law seems so abstract and formal, so concerned with fundamental political principles and entitlements, so legalistic, one might feel, that it is difficult to connect it to anything as mundane as the struggle of a gay teenager to find respect and understanding.

And yet, or so I shall contend, the domain of constitutional law has been, and continues to be, profoundly relevant for the politics of humanity—precisely *because* it concerns the most fundamental entitlements we all have as citizens, the most basic and general ways in which we make sense of our common political life and articulate its deepest purposes. Ideas such as the idea of the equal protection of the laws, or the idea of fundamental liberties, are abstract, but they are not lifeless. They are living realities, which must be duly articulated and made real in every citizen's life, if the words of the Constitution are to be more than idle talk.

One might agree with that idea and still doubt that "humanity," defined as involving not only respect, but also sympathetic imagination and responsiveness to the complexities of another's situation, is relevant to constitutional law. And yet, when cases reach the U.S. Supreme Court, they are usually legally difficult cases, to which formal legal analysis has suggested no unequivocal solution. In dealing with such cases, judges need to try to be human beings, seeking to understand the issues in their historical and cultural setting and with an eye to the human meanings they embody.[7] As we shall see, some of the Supreme Court cases dealing with sexual orientation show a remarkable moral obtuseness, involving a failure of basic human imagination. Others, however, show the Court attempting to grapple with human beings in their historical setting and to see the human meaning of the issues in question. I shall try to explain how a capacity for not just respect, but also for sympathy and imagination can, should, and occasionally does inform the lofty process of constitutional adjudication.

My own imagination on this topic was set to work by the man to whom I dedicate this book: the actor Herbert Foster, who for many years has played a wide range of roles in Shakespeare and other plays at the New York Public Theater. I met Herb when I was sixteen, a young apprentice actress in summer stock at the Berkshire Playhouse, where he was a featured professional actor. He was the first gay man I was aware that I knew, since I had led a very closeted life on Philadelphia's Main Line. (It seems right to speak of a closet of socially imposed ignorance about gay people, as well as a closet of personal concealment.) I was paired up with him in the ball scene in *My Fair Lady*; we danced together as Lord and Lady Tarrington (although he had other and more significant roles). I had a big crush on Herb, because he just seemed (and was) so much nicer than most of the other men around. (The theater, wonderful though it is, has its share of creeps.) When I realized he was gay, and met his partner, who came up on visits from New York, I was disappointed, but I also started thinking. I thought it so odd that the nicest person in the whole place should be in a position of semiconcealment, at least outside the "little world" of the theater (to use Ingmar Bergman's lovely term). I thought it would be nice if these two men, who had exchanged school rings in token of some type of commitment, could actually do what the straight men around them, however egotistical, or predatory, or emotionally frozen, could do any day. So I thought a lot about that, although Herb and I never spoke of this topic, and I later realized that he never knew I knew he was gay.

In 2008, reading about Herb's career on the net, I wrote him a letter telling him that I remembered him with pleasure, and I told him a little bit about my work, including my work on gay rights. He responded with a very warm letter and told me that he was gay (thus confirming the claim that the process of coming out never ends, since in this case it had taken forty-four years). He had broken up with that earlier partner long since, but for many years, he told me, he had had, and still has, a long-term happy relationship with someone else. Since they live in New York, which has decided to recognize same-sex unions legally contracted elsewhere, they now have the option that I imagined in 1964. I don't so much care whether they take it up—that is a profoundly personal matter, and my own views about it are mixed, as you will see. But I care that they have the same "capability" as others. The politics of equal respect already entails that equality of fundamental rights and opportunities. To get there, however, we first have to learn to think about one another with sympathy and imagination, and that is why we need something deeper and wider: the politics of humanity.

NOTES

1. Ritch Savin-Williams, "...*And Then I Became Gay": Young Men's Stories* (New York: Routledge, 1998), 52.

2. Ibid., 74–75.

3. Patrick Devlin, *The Enforcement of Morals* (London: Oxford University Press, 1965); Leon Kass, "The Wisdom of Repugnance: Why We Should Ban the Cloning of Human Beings," *New Republic* 216, issue 22 (June 2, 1997), 17–26; reprinted in Leon Kass and James Q. Wilson, eds., *The Ethics of Human Cloning* (Washington, DC: AEI Press, 1998), 3–60; related material is in chapter 5 of Kass's *Life, Liberty, and the Defense of Dignity: The Challenge for Bioethics* (San Francisco: Encounter Books, 2002).

4. This part of my analysis will draw on my *Hiding from Humanity: Disgust, Shame, and the Law* (Princeton: Princeton University Press, 2004).

5. See my "Objectification," in *Sex and Social Justice* (New York: Oxford University Press, 1999), 213–39.

6. Thus, in a famous passage of his *The Theory of Moral Sentiments* (Indianapolis, IN: Liberty Classics, 1976), Smith speaks of the response of a "man of humanity" in Europe to the news of an earthquake in China, where "humanity" designates the ability to imagine the catastrophe and its effects on the participants and to partake in their experience (136). A characteristic example of Cicero's usage is in a letter to Atticus about the unhappy marriage of his brother Quintus to Atticus's daughter Pomponia. After relating a marital spat, which, characteristically, Cicero wants to blame on Pomponia's insensitivity to her husband's situation and needs, he says, you see how lacking in *humanitas* she is?

7. See here the longer argument in my "Foreword: Constitutions and Capabilities: 'Perception' against Lofty Formalism," *Harvard Law Review* 121 (2007), 5–97.

FROM DISGUST TO HUMANITY

CHAPTER ONE

The Politics of Disgust: Practice, Theory, History

The typical sexual practices of homosexuals are a medical horror story—imagine exchanging saliva, feces, semen and/or blood with dozens of different men each year. Imagine drinking urine, ingesting feces and experiencing rectal trauma on a regular basis. Often these encounters occur while the participants are drunk, high, and/or in an orgy setting. Further, many of them occur in extremely unsanitary places (bathrooms, dirty peep shows), or, because homosexuals travel so frequently, in other parts of the world.

Every year, a quarter or more of homosexuals visit another country. Fresh American germs get taken to Europe, Africa, and Asia. And fresh pathogens from these continents come here. Foreign homosexuals regularly visit the U.S. and participate in this biological swapmeet.

—PAUL CAMERON,
MEDICAL CONSEQUENCES OF WHAT HOMOSEXUALS DO (PAMPHLET)

I. DISGUST IN PRACTICE: AMERICAN SEXUAL POLITICS

The American politics of sexual orientation, over the years, has been suffused with appeals to disgust. Crucial stages in our political evolution have been shaped by these appeals, just as our new emerging legal culture has been shaped by their rejection. Although we appear to be moving beyond this time, it is important to understand where we have come from, and why we should reject such a political approach.

Nor should we assume that the politics of disgust has disappeared. Like racism, disgust for gays and lesbians is now relatively unacceptable socially, at least in many contexts. That does not mean that it has stopped influencing the way people really think. Many inoffensive moral arguments that are put forward in this sphere may well be screens for darker motives. So we should understand disgust and its proponents as well as we can before describing the "politics of humanity" toward which we appear to be moving.

It's good to have a paradigm case to consider, so let us think about the work of Paul Cameron, founder and head of the Family Research Institute, which publishes voluminously on this topic and has submitted amicus briefs in several of the key gay rights cases. One of the most prolific and influential opponents of gay rights in today's America, Cameron has greatly influenced others who write or mobilize in this area, including Will Perkins, the primary proponent of Colorado's Amendment 2, the law that was declared unconstitutional by the U.S. Supreme Court in *Romer v. Evans*. Cameron was hired as consultant in the effort to craft Amendment 2, and he was later paid a large sum as consultant for the State of Colorado in the litigation after the amendment. Despite the fact that Cameron's views will seem extreme, at times even bizarre, it is good to be aware of their large political influence. Moreover, such views are probably much more influential than they appear to be: many people who would deny believing the things Cameron alleges, often sincerely, are likely to be influenced at a deeper level by the images of homosexuality he purveys.

Cameron's writings speak of "homosexuals," but in fact, with a few exceptions, they discuss only male homosexuality.[1] (This neglect of lesbians is typical of the group surrounding and influenced by Cameron: for example, Peter LaBarbera, president of Americans for Truth, writes about a gay event in San Francisco, "The Folsom Street Fair began as an event mainly for homosexual sadomasochists, but it now attracts many straights, as evidenced by the thousands of women visible at this year's event."[2])

When Cameron and his associates look at male homosexuality, they are virtually obsessed with the disgusting. Feces, saliva, urine, semen, blood—all these bodily products are harped on again and again in his writings, together with frequent references to dangerous disease-bearing germs. In the passage quoted above, Cameron first reduces the sexual practices of gay men to a set of (allegedly) disgusting bodily wastes. Then, for good measure, he links the acts to "unsanitary places." (But bathrooms are not inherently unsanitary. And peep shows, if dirty, are dirty in a metaphorical, not a literal, sense.) Finally, to the concoction is added a quintessentially American disgust-object: foreign germs. Gay men, apparently more than others, are travelers, taking American dirt to other nations and, worse by far, bringing foreign dirt back here. (Cameron here appropriates for his own purposes—without mentioning its source—an age-old stereotype of the Jew as homeless wanderer and "cosmopolitan," a stereotype, as we'll later see, intimately linked to the history of disgust as a political motive.[3])

Cameron is clearly more interested in arousing disgust than in rational analysis. He obsessively draws attention to the prominence of fellatio in male-male sexual encounters, and then writes, in a typical passage, "Semen contains many of the germs carried in the blood. Because of this, gays who practice oral sex verge on consuming raw human blood, with all its medical risks."[4] Never, however, does he pause to ask about the frequency of fellatio in heterosexual sex. (In this area there's a huge amount of bad faith, as people allege disgust at acts that are ubiquitous in heterosexual relations.) Nor does he inquire about the dangers of vaginal intercourse, where, according to his theory that semen is akin to raw blood, women receive raw human blood, "with all its medical risks." His fascination with the allegedly disgusting nature of anal intercourse neglects, equally, the fact that this practice is common among heterosexuals as well. (In some cultures, indeed, it is among the most common forms of contraception.[5])

Nor does Cameron offer any support for his contention that semen and urine are particularly "unsanitary." Urine in fact is sterile, unless a kidney or urinary tract infection is present. Nor is semen particularly germ-laden. As for blood, although many people find it alarming and even disgusting, it is not particularly germ-laden either. What makes the reception of a stranger's blood into one's veins dangerous is the possibility that it is the wrong blood type. This has nothing to do with receiving blood into one's mouth or stomach. Drinking human blood is per se no more dangerous than eating a rare steak. As for saliva, human saliva is indeed unusually germ filled—the reason why a human bite is usually treated as far more dangerous than a bite from a dog or cat. However, all this shows, if it shows anything, is that kissing, one of the most romanticized sex acts, is unusually "disgusting" and dangerous. Not surprisingly, Cameron fails to draw this conclusion.

Cameron appears particularly eager to describe, repeatedly, what he calls "fecal sex": "About 80% of gays," he writes, "admit to licking and/or inserting their tongues into the anus of partners and thus ingesting medically significant amounts of feces. Those who eat or wallow in it are probably at even greater risk."[6] "Fecal sex" combines the dirtiness of feces with the dirtiness of saliva. Because many people believe this act relatively rare among heterosexuals (although there are no reliable data), the example serves to exoticize the (allegedly) disgusting.

In one way, what Cameron appears to find disgusting, and wants the reader to find disgusting, is the everyday human body itself: its fluids, its excreta, its smells, its bloodiness—its animal nature, we might say. His rhetoric gets a toehold because most human beings are not fully comfortable about having an animal body. Fastening on aspects of the body that many if not most people view with discomfort, he hypes them up into something truly revolting and threatening. On the other hand, however, Cameron assuages this discomfort by saying: that disgusting stuff is over there, in the body of the gay man. It is not in you and your intimate relationships. Straights don't ejaculate, their blood never contaminates the bodies of others with dangerous substances, their kisses are germ free. The intended reader is revolted, but at the same time comforted: I am nothing like this, nor does my sex life have any connection with this.

Cameron's rhetoric has a dual goal: to inspire simple revulsion and loathing for gay men, and to link their practices to disease and danger. Thus hepatitis B and HIV/AIDS are often mentioned as likely consequences of the allegedly disgusting behavior. The appeal to fear of disease itself contains a further appeal to disgust: for the diseases are described as borne by "germs" and "pathogens," so that the viewer has the picture of revolting bugs crawling out of the body of the gay man and onto their own (allegedly clean) bodies. Indeed, homosexuality itself soon becomes one of those disgusting bugs: "Homosexuality," he writes, "is an infectious appetite with personal and social consequences."[7]

Cameron often denounces the alleged promiscuity of gay men; but the monogamous fare no better. One of his arguments against the legalization of same-sex marriage is that men in monogamous

[5]

relationships are more likely to engage in "dirty" and "unsafe" practices such as sex without condoms. Gay marriage, he concludes, is "a health hazard." "Not only does it place homosexuals at increased risk for HIV and other sexually transmitted diseases, but it also subjects them to an increased threat of domestic violence and early death."

Cameron dresses up his studies with tables, charts, and statistics, publishing articles in "academic" journals that are invented by his own group or affiliated groups.[8] He also heads a privately funded institute, the Institute for the Scientific Investigation of Sexuality (ISIS), which purports to do nationwide sociological research. He has, however, no scientific standing. He has been cast out of both the American Psychological Association and the American Sociological Association (ASA), and his studies have been repeatedly denounced as mere propaganda masquerading as science. The ASA wrote, "Dr. Cameron has consistently misinterpreted and misrepresented sociological research on sexuality, homosexuality, and lesbianism." Not one of his studies has been published in a respected scientific journal with rigorous review standards. Nonetheless, Cameron's writings continue to be cited ubiquitously in the struggle to limit gay rights, and are often cited even by courts. In 2003, his research was cited by the dissenters in the Massachusetts Supreme Court case that led to the legalization of same-sex marriage. In 2004, he was cited by the Florida Supreme Court in a case that upheld a law banning adoption by same-sex couples.[9]

What does Cameron want? In the first place, he seeks to prevent the legalization of same-sex marriage and to put an end to nondiscrimination laws protecting gays and lesbians. His work was the inspiration for pamphlets circulated during the campaign on behalf of Amendment 2 in Colorado, saying that gay men eat feces and drink raw blood, and he personally campaigned against a nondiscrimination ordinance in Lincoln, Nebraska. Cameron also clearly favored sodomy laws, when those were still on the books. "Destroy the homosexual infrastructure," said an exhibit put up by his organization; "Punish homosexual acts." He has suggested, moreover, that the right to travel might be revoked for homosexuals: the same exhibit said, "Stop the pipeline: Cut homosexual travel."[10]

Cameron's rhetoric, however, suggests yet more ominous ideas. According to the Associated Press, he said in 1987, "Screen and quarantine until we come up with a cure. Rights have run amok in our society, particularly sexual ones. Homosexuals were hung 300 years ago in our society." In 1994, his sidekick, the Rev. Bill Banuchi, executive director of the New York chapter of the Christian Coalition, said that gays should be legally required to wear warning labels, like those on cigarette packs—or, we might add, like the pink triangles gays had to wear under the Nazi regime, now a symbol of gay pride.[11]

Cameron is extreme, and though his brand of extremism has been and is highly influential, what seems more important is that he represents an extreme version of something very widespread. As we'll see, the discomfort people feel about their smelly, decaying, and all-too-mortal bodies has ubiquitously and monotonously been projected outward onto groups who can serve as, so to speak, the surrogate dirt of a community, enabling the dominant group to feel clean and heavenly. For many people in America, gay men provoke such disgust-projections, particularly in (straight) men. Even well-intentioned liberals may feel overwhelming disgust when thinking about gay male sex acts, or when thinking that a gay man is looking at them with the fantasy of performing such acts. Thus Cameron cannily taps into a widespread cultural phenomenon in the United States, which he exploits and magnifies.

Disgust-anxiety is far from the only factor influencing policies hostile to the full equality of gays and lesbians in American life. Many arguments are put forward in connection with specific issues

[7]

(such as the Colorado nondiscrimination ordinance or the issue of same-sex marriage); some of them look like rational arguments. I shall argue, however, that these arguments on their own do not justify the conclusions their proponents draw—sometimes because they rest on false claims (about same-sex families, child molestation, etc.), sometimes because they simply don't justify as strong a conclusion as their proponents wish to draw from them. The appeal to disgust, sometimes covert and sometimes all too evident, has been a crucial part of the antigay strategy.

2. DISGUST IN THEORY: DEVLIN AND KASS

How might widespread disgust toward a group help to justify laws that disadvantage that group? At first one might suppose that there is no connection, and I shall argue that this is in fact correct. Disgust, however, has been prominently defended as a legitimate, even a central, source for law. Before we think about why it might not be a legitimate or reliable source, then, we ought to try to understand the arguments of its defenders.

The two most prominent defenders of disgust as a criterion for the legal regulation of conduct are Lord Patrick Devlin, a British lawyer, eventually a "Law Lord" who wrote influentially about disgust and law in the 1950s, and Leon Kass, an American bioethicist who is a professor at the University of Chicago and who was chair of the President's Council on Bioethics from 2002 to 2005. The arguments of Devlin and Kass are rather different, but both conclude that widespread disgust at a practice is sufficient reason to forbid that practice through law, even if it involves only consenting parties and does not violate the rights of the nonconsenting. Devlin's central target was the proposed decriminalization of consenting same-sex sexual acts. Kass focuses on the prospect of human cloning, but he suggests that his strictures would apply to a wide range of other practices, including same-sex acts.

Devlin's well-known essays on public morality were written in opposition to the 1957 report of the Wolfenden Commission, which recommended abolishing legal penalties for consenting homosexual acts between adults.[12] He agreed with the commission that personal liberty is an important social value that should not be curtailed in the absence of a strong public interest. He argued, however, that any society that is going to survive needs an "established morality" that is broadly shared. The "loosening of moral bonds" is often a sign of social "disintegration." Society is therefore "justified in taking the same steps to preserve its moral code as it does to preserve its government and other essential institutions." To illustrate the idea of "disintegration," Devlin cited the dangers of widespread drunkenness and drug abuse. These "vices," he argued, would prevent society from rallying to ward off an enemy attack: "[a] nation of debauchees would not in 1940 have responded satisfactorily to Winston Churchill's call to blood and toil and sweat and tears."[13] For Devlin, homosexuals are "debauchees"; they are "addicts," whose immersion in sex is incompatible with being a reliable citizen. (He never offered any argument to support his view that homosexuals are more addicted to sex than heterosexuals.) He concluded that homosexual acts are like drug use: both should be criminalized, because protection of a shared moral code is necessary in order to prevent a social shipwreck.

Not all threats to a society's moral code are sufficient to justify legal intervention, Devlin argued. We need a test to determine when the point has been reached beyond which society should not tolerate immoral conduct for the sake of liberty. Because Devlin viewed immorality as like an infection, weakening the body politic, he was unwilling to adopt John Stuart Mill's principle that only the imminent prospect of harm to others licenses restrictive laws.

Conduct between consenting adults can undermine social solidarity by weakening the grip of the established morality. Since Devlin was unwilling to look to harm as the test for legal regulability, he needed a different sort of criterion to identify when the point of regulability has been reached. Disgust, because it is a very intense form of disapproval, provides him with such a test. When an average member of society—Devlin called this person "the man on the Clapham omnibus"[14]—feels disgust at the thought of some behavior that does not directly affect him, we may conclude that this conduct is "a vice so abominable that its mere presence is an offence."

In other words, Devlin was not talking about cases in which disgust is elicited by an actual homosexual solicitation. Nor was he talking about public conduct, which might directly cause offense to its viewers. He was talking about what the Wolfenden Report proposed to decriminalize—private, consensual sex acts. He imagined that the man on the Clapham omnibus feels disgust at the mere thought that such acts are going on in his society. When such an intense reaction is present, we are entitled to restrict personal liberty by making laws against the conduct that provokes it. The reason for the restriction is not paternalistic, for the sake of "improving" the lives of those who are living "badly." It is, rather, self-protective: society defends itself by punishing those who violate conventional moral norms.

Leon Kass's argument is different from Devlin's.[15] Devlin was a Burkean conservative: he relied on disgust because it seemed to him to be an expression of deep-seated social conventions. Like Devlin, Kass dislikes the Millian idea that people should be free to choose their own conduct, so long as it does no harm to others. He calls this a world "in which everything is held to be permissible so long as it is freely done, in which our given human nature no longer commands respect." Unlike Devlin, however, Kass has no particular respect for convention as such. But he believes that disgust is a reliable warning sign, steering us away from atrocity. It is unclear how he thinks this mechanism works, but the most likely reading is that he believes human nature to be purposively designed (perhaps by God) in such a way that its visceral responses give us important information about what is good for us. Disgust thus contains a "wisdom" that lies beneath all rational argument. It "revolts against the excesses of human willfulness, warning us not to transgress what is unspeakably profound."[16]

Devlin and Kass both fail to confront squarely the consequences of their positions. Societies have felt strong disgust toward many people and practices, including members of lower castes and classes, foreigners, people with disabilities, people with physical deformities, Jews, and people who contract interracial marriages. Either they ought to say that such disgust is a reliable legal criterion, sufficient to permit us to saddle these people with legal prohibitions or disadvantages, or they ought to introduce some further distinctions. The former course would not satisfy most fair-minded people. But they clearly do not take the latter course either, since they do not provide any further distinctions, but only some examples that, by themselves, do not show the pertinence of disgust as a legal criterion. Devlin confined his examples to addicts, including alcoholics, drug addicts, and homosexuals (imagined as sex addicts). Kass cites a wide range of examples where there is actual harm inflicted on a nonconsenting party (parent-child incest, bestiality, rape, murder, and cannibalism, which is usually preceded by murder). An obvious problem with all of these examples is that there is no need to appeal to disgust to give an account of their wrongfulness. In fact, these cases would be regulated by a Millian, because the rights of others are violated; thus they cannot serve as counterexamples to Mill's idea that harm is a necessary condition of legal regulability.[17] Nor does Kass confront cases like those I have listed above, in which disgust (at least at some times in some places) would suggest legal regulation, but where we now feel that such regulation would be unjust. It is here that he would have to make his case, because he would have to deal with the fact that disgust suggests conclusions that are out of step with what we now think right. Instead, however, he merely jumps ahead in the argument and applies his conclusion to the case that interests him, human cloning, suggesting that our (allegedly) widespread disgust at the thought of this practice is sufficient reason to make it illegal.

Indeed, Kass does not even confront obvious difficulties for his thesis raised by everyday experience. Small children, when they first learn the facts of heterosexual sex, are usually disgusted—perhaps because they don't like being confronted with the bodily reality of their parents, having thought of their parents as superhuman figures, or perhaps just because all those bodily fluids are just disgusting to them in a primary way. (It is very difficult to know whether this disgust is primary-object disgust or projective disgust.) For Kass, this spells real difficulty, given that the central sexual case that he would like to uphold as paradigmatic of the normal, the moral, and the good is the procreative sexuality of that child's parents. Similarly problematic is the fact that many common medical procedures (colonoscopies, open heart surgery, etc.) are commonly regarded as disgusting—and yet we have never even contemplated regulating these procedures out of loyalty to our sense of disgust.

At one point Kass expresses concern about the way in which "some of yesterday's repugnances are today calmly accepted—though, one must add, not always for the better."[18] Because I know of no reason to think that Kass opposes miscegenation, grieves for the demise of the Indian caste system, favors anti-Semitic laws, or supports legal inequality for people with disabilities, it seems likely that he is referring to homosexual relations, which he strongly opposes. But he does not help us distinguish the case of homosexual relations from those other cases; he does not tell us why disgust has simply disappeared, if it is in fact so reliable; and he does not give us any assistance in distinguishing the type of disgust that may be pertinent to law from types that are more evanescent and less pertinent. In short, Devlin and Kass do not argue well. That does not prove, however, that they are wrong. (Indeed, one of Devlin's points is that we should not base law on reason alone: he explicitly claims that we should turn lawmaking over to forces that lie beneath rational argument.) Certainly what they say resonates with prominent aspects of people's emotional lives. People do feel deep disgust with certain practices and, by extension, the groups that engage in those practices. They believe that these practices threaten the social fabric, and they are usually eager to make law in response to that perceived threat. A closer investigation of the emotion of disgust is therefore needed, before we can conclude that it is inappropriate for a liberal democratic society to rely on this emotion as a source of law.

3. DISGUST: AN UNRELIABLE EMOTION

Disgust appears to be an especially visceral emotion.[19] We readily grant that emotions such as compassion, grief, and anger are affected by social learning. What are significant losses? Which people should we care about? What damages is it right to be upset about? All these questions form part of children's upbringing in their social environment, and the social norms they learn in the process of investigating these questions powerfully shape the child's emotions. Thus if children learn that animals are brutes who do not suffer, they will be unlikely to feel compassion for the plight of animals raised for food in confining conditions. If members of a group believe that they ought to have rights and privileges less extensive than those of the dominant group, they will be slow to feel angry at their subordination. (Such absence of anger has long been an integral part of the subordination of women.) Disgust, however, seems different: it seems like a deep-seated bodily response to certain smells, sights, and feels, which has little to do with what we learn or how we interpret the world.

In the past twenty years, however, important experimental work by psychologist Paul Rozin and his colleagues has shown conclusively that disgust has a marked cognitive element.[20] What people find disgusting depends crucially on the idea they have of the object. Thus disgust is not simple sensory distaste. Subjects who sniff the same odor from two vials, being told that one contains feces and the other contains cheese, are usually disgusted by the first but not by the second. Nor is disgust identical with the sense of danger. People will eat formerly poisonous mushrooms if they are convinced that all the poison has been removed, but they won't swallow a cockroach even if they are sure it has been sterilized; subjects even refuse to swallow a cockroach sealed in a plastic capsule that will emerge, undigested, in the subject's feces.[21]

Disgust, Rozin finds, concerns the borders of the body. Its central idea is that of contamination: the disgusted person feels defiled by the object, thinking that it has somehow entered the self. Further experiments show that behind this idea of personal contamination lies the idea that "you are what you eat": if you take in something base or vile, you become like that yourself.

So what are people unwilling to be or become? The so-called primary objects of disgust are reminders of human animality and mortality: feces, other bodily fluids, corpses, and animals or insects who have related properties (slimy, smelly, oozy). Rozin concludes that it is the filth and stench of humanity itself that underlies all of disgust's more parochial instances. Not all aspects of our animality are disgusting: strength and speed, for example.[22] Those that are loathed are those that are connected to death and decay.

When people experience disgust, then, they are expressing an aversion to prominent aspects of what every human being is. They feel contaminated by what reminds them of these aspects, which people often prefer to conceal. Such aversions almost certainly have an evolutionary basis, but they still have to be confirmed by learning: children do not exhibit disgust until the ages of two to three years old, during the time of toilet training. This means that society has room to interpret and shape the emotion, directing it to some objects rather than others, as happens with anger and compassion.

In virtually all societies, disgust is standardly felt toward a group of *primary objects*: feces, blood, semen, urine, nasal discharges, menstrual discharges, corpses, decaying meat, and animals/insects that are oozy, slimy, or smelly. (Rozin finds that although blood is not experienced as disgusting when it is inside one's own body, it becomes disgusting after it leaves it; the same appears to be true of breast milk, which many people, including mothers themselves, find disgusting to drink.) Tears would appear to be the one human bodily secretion that is not generally found disgusting—perhaps because, being uniquely human, tears do not remind us of our links with the rest of the animal kingdom. Primary-object disgust does not entirely track the dangerous: we aren't disgusted by pathogens that we don't see, and we are disgusted by substances that are just slimy, oozy, or smelly but not dangerous. Nonetheless, disgust at primary objects is usually a useful heuristic, steering us away from the dangerous when there is no time for detailed inquiry.

Disgust is then extended from object to object in ways that could hardly bear rational scrutiny. This sort of extended disgust is what I call *projective disgust*. Rozin calls the principles of disgust-projection "laws of sympathetic magic." One such magical idea is that if object A is disgusting and B looks like A, B is also disgusting. Thus, subjects refuse to eat soup stirred with a sterile flyswatter, or to drink liquid from a sterile bedpan. Another magical idea is that of contagion: objects that have touched each other never cease to act on one another. Thus, after a dead cockroach is dropped into a glass of juice people refuse to drink that *type* of juice afterward. Well-washed clothing that has been worn by someone with an infectious disease is rejected, and some people refuse all secondhand clothing.

Projective disgust is shaped by social norms, as societies teach their members to identify alleged contaminants in their midst. All societies, it appears, identify at least some humans as disgusting. Very likely this is a stratagem adopted to cordon off the dominant group more securely from its own feared animality: if those quasi humans stand between me and the world of disgusting animality, then I am that much further from being mortal/decaying/smelly/oozy myself. Projective disgust rarely has any reliable connection with genuine danger. It feeds on fantasy, and engineers subordination. Although it does serve a deep-seated human need—the need to represent oneself as pure and others as dirty—this is a need whose relation to social fairness looks (and is) highly questionable.

Projective disgust (involving projection of disgust properties onto a group or individual) takes many forms, but it always involves linking the allegedly disgusting group or person somehow with the primary objects of disgust. Sometimes this is done by stressing the close practical connection of the group with the primary objects: untouchables in the Indian caste system were those who cleaned latrines and disposed of corpses; women seem to many men to be particularly closely linked with blood and other bodily fluids through their receptive sexuality, their role in birth, and menstruation, a common source of norms of "untouchability."

Often, however, the extension works in more fantasy-laden ways, by imputing to people or groups properties similar to those that are found disgusting in the primary objects: bad smell, ooziness, rotten-ness, germiness, decay. Typically, these projections have no basis in reality. Jews are not really slimy, or similar to maggots, although German anti-Semites, and Hitler himself, said that they were. African-Americans do not smell worse than other human beings, although racists said that they did. And often, even when there is an element of what I've called practical connection, projection imputes dirtiness or contamination where there is no reason to do so. Gandhi observed, for example, that "untouchables" were actually cleaner in their habits than upper castes, and thus at lower risk of contracting cholera: they defecated in the fields, far from their dwellings, whereas upper castes used chamber pots that were then emptied into the gutters outside their windows. Notice, then, that projective disgust involves a double fantasy: a fantasy of the dirtiness of the other and a fantasy of one's own purity. Both sides of the projection involve false belief, and both conduce to a politics of hierarchy.

Societies have many ways of stigmatizing vulnerable minorities.[23] Disgust is not the only mechanism of stigmatization. It is, however, a powerful and central one, and when it is removed (when, for example, aversion to physical contact with a racial minority is no longer present), other modes of hierarchy tend to depart along with it.

It is not surprising that sexuality is an area of life in which disgust often plays a role. Sex involves the exchange of bodily fluids, and it marks us as bodily beings rather than angelic transcendent beings. So sex is a site of anxiety for anyone who is ambivalent about having an animal and mortal nature, and that includes many if not most people. Primary-object disgust therefore plays a significant role in sexual relations, as the bodily substances people encounter in sex (semen, sweat, feces, menstrual blood) are very often found disgusting and seen as contaminants. Therefore, it is not surprising that projective disgust also plays a prominent role in the sexual domain. In almost all societies, people identify a group of sexual actors as disgusting or pathological, contrasting them with "normal" or "pure" sexual actors (prominently including the people themselves and their own group). This stigmatization takes many different forms. Misogyny is an aspect of it in most cultures, as males distance themselves from the discomfort they feel by associating bodily fluids with the woman who receives them, and not, at the same time, with their own bodies.[24] Derogatory portrayals of women as disgusting (smelly, oozy, full of questionable fluids) are used by men to distance themselves from their own animality. Indeed, as the point was vividly, albeit extremely, made by the influential German theorist Otto Weininger at the start of the twentieth century, woman (in this cultural fantasy) is simply the body of the man, "his other, ineradicable, his lower part."[25] Notice, here again, the double fantasy—of the other's dirt and one's own purity, both supported by a kind of wishful thinking and both conducing to a politics of subordination.

Beyond this, societies have varied in the groups of sexual actors whom they identify as disgusting. I shall argue later that gay men have not always been disgust objects for heterosexual men. In what we might call yesterday's America however—meaning a very recent time from which we are slowly moving away—there is no doubt that the body of the gay man has been a central locus of disgust-anxiety—above all, for other men. Female homosexuals may be objects of fear, or moral indignation, or generalized anxiety; but they have less often been objects of disgust. Similarly, heterosexual females may have felt negative emotions toward the male homosexual—fear, moral indignation, anxiety—but again, they have more rarely felt emotions of disgust.

Since this sort of disgust is still prevalent, though perhaps less so than in the past, we may now use the present tense as we investigate it. What inspires disgust is typically the male thought of the male homosexual, imagined as anally penetrable. The idea of semen and feces mixing together inside the body of a male is one of the most disgusting ideas imaginable—to males, for whom the idea of nonpenetrability is a sacred boundary against stickiness, ooze, and death. (The idea of contamination-by-penetration is probably one central idea, but the more general idea is that of the male body as defiled by the contamination of bodily fluids: and proximity to a contaminated body is itself contaminating.) The presence of a homosexual male in the neighborhood inspires the thought that one might lose one's own clean safeness, one might become the receptacle for those animal products. Thus disgust is ultimately disgust at one's own imagined penetrability and ooziness, and this is why the male homosexual is both regarded with disgust and viewed with fear as a predator who might make everyone else disgusting. The very look of such a male is itself contaminating—as we see in the extraordinary debates about showers in the military. The gaze of a homosexual male is seen as contaminating because it says, "You can be penetrated." And this means that you can be made of feces and semen and blood, not clean plastic flesh. Thus it is not surprising that (to males) the thought of homosexual sex is even more disgusting than the thought of reproductive sex, despite the strong connection of the latter with mortality and the cycle of the generations. For in heterosexual sex the male imagines that not he but a lesser being (the woman, seen as animal) receives the pollution of bodily fluids; in imagining homosexual sex he is forced to imagine that he himself might be so polluted. This inspires a stronger need for boundary drawing.

Such are the deep and widespread anxieties tapped, and heightened, by Paul Cameron and his allies. Important recent research demonstarates that theere is a strong correlation between disgust-sensitivity and anti-gay attitudes, particularly attitudes about gay sex and same-sex marriage.[26] Cameron's canny addition of germs and the viral contamination of HIV to the mix makes his disgust-rhetoric especially powerful in the United States, a very health-focused and germ-phobic nation.

Sometimes the appeal to disgust provides extra support for policies that are defensible in other more pertinent terms. For example, we are disgusted by the idea of eating dog meat; but bans on the raising of dogs for food can be defended without alluding to that reaction, by pointing to the cruelty to dogs, which is already illegal in itself.[27] We could, then, sometimes rely on disgust without losing our grip on harm, and even while mobilizing opposition to harm. My contention is, however, that contamination of the self, the evil toward which disgust is directed, is a harm pertinent to legal regulation only when we are talking about contamination that is a real harm, for example being forced to live next door to a running sewer. As we'll see, this type of disgust at primary objects rightly plays a limited role in the law, providing part of the content of the law of nuisance (see chapters 3 and 6).[28]

In "projective disgust," by contrast, the contamination is not literal and physical, but imaginary; as we've seen, the projection of disgust properties onto subordinate groups is a common way of stigmatizing them as sick and inferior, and the fantasies that mediate that extension cannot withstand rational scrutiny. I contend that projective disgust plays no proper role in arguing for legal regulation, because of the emotion's normative irrationality and its connection to stigma and hierarchy.

We cannot conclude that a policy is wrong simply because it is backed by a rhetoric of disgust: for there may be other better reasons in its favor. Disgust, however, often prevents us from looking for those good reasons, creating the misleading impression that the policy has already been well defended. Turning to it to legitimize policies that can be defended in other ways is therefore dangerous, because this encourages us to stop short in our search for rationally defensible categories. And the emotion itself encourages us to accept hierarchies and boundaries that are not defensible within a political tradition based on equal respect.

Even those who believe that disgust still provides a sufficient reason for rendering certain practices illegal, however, should agree with a weaker thesis: namely, that disgust provides no good reason for limiting liberties or compromising equalities that are constitutionally protected.

4. DISGUST IN HISTORY: STIGMA AND SUBORDINATION

Scientific research on disgust gives us strong reasons to doubt its suitability as a basis for lawmaking. Disgust at primary objects at least tracks real danger to some extent, and insofar as it does, it gives reasons for laws (concerning sanitation, the disposal of corpses, etc.) protecting citizens from objects that disgust rightly identifies as harmful. Such is not the case, however, with projective disgust. The connection of this sort of disgust with self-loathing, its extension through laws of "sympathetic magic," and its tendency to impute to others properties that are present but not confronted in the self, all make it look irrational in a normative sense, riddled with inconsistency, eager to scapegoat others for one's own human weakness. Individual cases of anger, fear, and compassion may be misplaced if they are based on false beliefs about what happened or on indefensible social norms about what is worth taking seriously. Projective disgust (the sort that is at issue in social debates about homosexuality) looks different, because its key cases always involve something like self-loathing or self-deception—or a refusal to face that which one is. We might, then, doubt the Leon Kass thesis that disgust contains an illuminating sort of "wisdom."

We have not yet answered Devlin, however, because Devlin does not base his defense of disgust on the claim that it gives us moral insight. He focuses only on social stability, claiming that if we follow the promptings of the disgust of the average person, we will protect society from disintegration. To answer Devlin, we may now turn to history, looking at some of the ways in which reliance on disgust has worked socially. More or less invariably, it has enabled a dominant group to subordinate the powerless. If this is stability (and such arrangements can indeed be stable), it is not the sort of stability that a liberal-democratic society, based on the idea of the equal worth of every citizen, should pursue.

History provides us with countless cases of disgust-based subordination. We have already seen the role disgust plays in men's domination of women. Let us now consider just two further cases, to which we have already alluded: the Indian caste hierarchy, and German anti-Semitism.

According to long-standing Hindu traditions, a wide range of people used to be categorized as "untouchable." Included in this group were people whose occupations (cleaning latrines, disposing of corpses) put them in regular contact with disgust's primary objects. Even though there is no rational path from that occupation to the idea that the person is filthy and polluted (as Gandhi pointed out), we can at least understand why the connection arose. The category, however, included many others whose connection to filth was merely magical or symbolic, people who performed a wide range of occupations; many *dalits*,[29] for example, are agricultural laborers. For some time, and today, the only reliable way to identify a *dalit* is by the last name. All over India, people know those names, and in an instant they identify the *dalit* in this way.[30] Nonetheless, given the power of fantasy, people really believed that the touch of such a person was dirty and polluting, and many probably still do believe this. People refused to accept food prepared or served by such a person. Marriage to such a person was, and in most quarters still is, utterly unthinkable. (Similar ideas of stigma and pollution played a central role in racism directed against African-Americans, as the exclusion of such people from swimming pools and drinking fountains, and the ban on miscegenation, attest.)

Being far away from such ideas in time and place, we easily see that they are both irrational in the normative sense, based on no good reasons, and deeply harmful. It seems entirely correct that the practices associated with untouchability were put off-limits by the Indian constitution, even though they were once central in Hindu religion. Disgust exhibited not wisdom but horrible violence against human dignity. The social order it sustained may have been stable, but it was hierarchical, unjust, and unworthy of a nation committed to the ideas of equal dignity and worth.

Now consider the second example. It may seem too easy to impugn disgust by associating it with Nazism, but I choose this illustration largely because there is so much good scholarship about it; the same conclusions could be shown through many other examples. The stock image of the Jew, in anti-Semitic propaganda in Germany from the Middle Ages on, depicted the Jew as disgusting in a variety of ways. Typically Jews were characterized as in essence "female," and various properties related to the debased category of the female were then imputed to them: bad smell, stickiness, uncleanness. The influential German sex theorist Otto Weininger wrote a whole chapter arguing that the Jew was in fact a woman, contrasting both Jews and women to the clean transcendent self of the German male. The Nazis developed these images even further, portraying Jews as disgusting insects or other vile animals, and also as germs, cancer cells, and "fungoid growths." The German male body was characterized as clean and hard, but the Jew could enter it, contaminate it, and cause it to rot. (For Hitler, the Jew was "a maggot inside a rotting body.") German depictions of the Jew lie very close to Paul Cameron's depictions of gay men, because they invoke core disgust-ideas, mingled with ideas of contagion and degeneration. Once again, we can see, looking back at history, how irrational these projections were, and how much harm they did.

[23]

These examples don't prove that disgust is always irrational and harmful. But when we combine these prominent cases with the experiment-based analysis of disgust's content and workings, we have very strong reasons to resist Devlin's thesis and any thesis like his. The psychological analysis already showed that Kass is wrong: disgust is not wise but terribly obtuse. The historical cases show that great harm to human dignity is frequently done by reliance on disgust as a source of law, and that the social solidarity it creates is often poisonous. When we combine the cases with the analysis, we have good reason to think that these harms recur with monotonous regularity: projective disgust is inspired by a powerful loathing of aspects of the self, and it typically seeks a handy scapegoat. The idea of subordinating others by imputing disgust-properties to them lies at the heart of disgust's dynamics.

Cameron (and his allies) may respond by arguing that disgust at male homosexuals and their acts is different, because it is natural and ineliminable. History shows us, however, that disgust at a group typically seems natural to those brought up to feel it. The Indian caste system was perpetuated for centuries precisely because it seemed natural, and even today its images of taint and stigma continue to exercise a powerful influence—despite the fact that nobody who enters the culture from outside can understand why it should make any difference that someone's last name is Thorat or Ambedkar, rather than Chatterjee or Bagchi.[31] As often, so here: culture feels like nature.

Moreover, in many cultures, past and present, men who regularly performed same-sex acts were not objects of disgust. Ancient Greece was not a society free of disgust. Oral sex, for example, was typically thought disgusting and stigmatizing for both parties (but especially the receptive party). Sex between men, however, while surrounded with many ethical rules and caveats, was not thought to be per se foul or loathsome. Indeed, it was generally believed that the gods themselves greatly enjoyed such acts.[32] The fact that the Greeks thought or did something does not make that thing good, but it ought to make us think. Insofar as we admire the Greeks and consider them a successful culture, we have reason to reflect about the difference between their disgust-reactions and our own, especially when we make claims about the social decay that an acceptance of same-sex relationships would bring.

Many nations in the modern world also now appear to have the view that same-sex acts are not disgusting. Most of the nations of Western Europe think this way.[33] This is even more relevant to our reflections, because these nations share a Christian religious heritage with us, so we can see that our own politics of sexual orientation is not dictated simply by the nature of that heritage. Contemporary Christians, even those who think of themselves as fundamentalist, disregard statements in the Bible all the time. For example, the Bible devotes much more space to punishing the evils of fortune-telling than to the evils of homosexuality—treated in half a sentence in Leviticus, which makes no reference to women and targets only some male-male sex acts. Modern Christians do not seek laws punishing fortune-telling. Similarly, greed is the object of far more energetic invective in the Bible than any sexual sin, but modern Christians generally do not seek to punish greed. Europe is illuminating for us because its difference from us reminds us that we have made a selective use of our Biblical heritage. We should ask ourselves why we have made the choices we have.

Why, then, do antigay attitudes play such a large part in American politics? This is a difficult question. We might mention Americans' disproportionate anxiety about illness, death, and decay. But these factors don't fully explain why disgust is so prominent a part of people's dealings with gays and lesbians, and gay men in particular. We might add that Americans characteristically exhibit a lot of anxiety about sexual variety, perhaps even about sex itself, and are, in many ways, less tolerant sexually than are people in many European nations.[34] Perhaps this explains why there is such a high level of disgust-anxiety in the sexual domain. Certainly, reflecting on stereotypes of masculinity as transcendence and impermeability helps us understand why the gay man seems so threatening to many other American men.

But such speculation is not the primary concern of this book. What is most important for our purposes is that projective disgust seems a bad source of law in a nation of equals, given its links with irrational fantasy and its tendency to establish unjust hierarchies.

How powerful is disgust today in antigay politics? Disgust is like racial hatred: it does not always announce itself in polite company. Paul Cameron appeals to disgust in a frank and open way, and he remains influential in certain circles. But many people who support his causes use other arguments: opposition to "special rights," concerns about alleged dangers to children, concerns about "public morality," the worry that heterosexual marriage will be debased. We shall pursue those arguments in later chapters. What we'll find, though, is that either they are too flimsy to do much work without disgust as a backdrop, or they are merely a mask for the politics of disgust.

NOTES

1. He once does claim, however, that statistics support the conclusion that lesbians are three hundred times more likely than heterosexual women to die in car accidents. The life expectancy of lesbians in America, he elsewhere claims, is only forty-five years (as contrasted with about eighty years for straight women).

2. Peter LaBarbera and Allyson Smith, "Tolerance Gone Wild in San Francisco as Cops Stand By Amidst Folsom Street Fair's Public Perversions and Widespread Nudity," October 2007, www.americansfortruth.org, http://americansfortruth.com/news/tolerance-gone-wild-in-san-francisco-as-cops-stand-by-amidst-folsom-street-fairs-public-perversions-and-widespread-nudity.html.

3. See also Cameron, "Effect of Homosexuality upon Public Health and Social Order," *Psychological Reports* 64 (1989), 1167–79, in which he claims that one quarter of Danish homosexuals have had sex "either with visiting USA homosexuals or during visits to the USA during the past year," and links this alleged behavior with the intercontinental spread of a variety of diseases, from HIV to amoebiasis.

4. Cameron, "Medical Consequences of What Homosexuals Do," (Colorado Springs, CO: Family Research Institute), distributed as a pamphlet and online at http://www.familyresearchinst.org/2009/02/medical-consequences-of-what-homosexuals-do/.

5. See Kenneth J. Dover, *Greek Homosexuality*, 2nd ed. (Cambridge, MA: Harvard University Press, 1986), which shows that a large proportion of the vase paintings of heterosexual intercourse in ancient Greece depict anal intercourse.

6. Cameron, "Medical Consequences."

7. Cameron, quoted in David Holthouse, "The Fabulist," Intelligence Report of the Southern Poverty and Law Center, Winter 2005 (Montgomery, AL); http://www.splcenter.org/intel/intelreport/article.jsp?aid=587.

8. *Psychological Reports* appears to be in essence a vanity press. All authors are required to pay a range of fees for the publication of their articles, usually around $27.00 per page; allegedly those charges are for "preprints" of the articles, but it is not standard journal policy to require authors to purchase offprints or preprints, so this is in effect a charge for publication.

9. Holthouse, "The Fabulist."

10. Ibid.

11. Ibid.

12. Devlin's various lectures on the topic are gathered under the title of the most famous one: *The Enforcement of Morals* (London: Oxford University Press, 1965). Devlin's position about homosexual acts is actually complex: he favored retention of the more serious criminal offense of "buggery" (anal intercourse between men), but favored the abolition of a more recent law, enacted in 1885, prohibiting "gross indecency" between

men, unless committed toward an underage youth. His argument was that focusing on "buggery" ensures that only "clear and flagrant" cases will be prosecuted (v–vi).

13. Devlin, *Enforcement of Morals*, 111. The cruel falsity of Devlin's claim that gays cannot defend their country is shown by the life and death of Alan Turing, who contributed immeasurably to Britain's victory by cracking the Enigma code, perhaps shortening the war by two years. Turing spent much of his life being hounded by the police for consensual homosexual sex; he was convicted under the Gross Indecency Act and sentenced to undergo hormone "therapy." He died, possibly as a suicide, shortly before Devlin published his book.

14. Ibid., 15.

15. Leon Kass, "The Wisdom of Repugnance: Why We Should Ban the Cloning of Human Beings," *New Republic* 216, issue 22 (June 2, 1997), 17–26; reprinted in *The Ethics of Human Cloning*, ed. Leon Kass and James Q. Wilson, eds., *The Ethics of Human Cloning* (Washington, DC: AEI Press, 1998), 3–60, p. at p. 19 in the latter pagination.

16. Ibid.

17. See Kass, "Wisdom of Repugnance," 18–19.

18. Ibid., 18.

19. The discussion in this section is closely related to the longer analysis in my book *Hiding from Humanity: Disgust, Shame, and the Law* (Princeton: Princeton University Press, 2004), chap. 2.

20. Rozin's publications are voluminous, but see, in particular, "Disgust," in *Handbook of Emotions*, 2nd ed., ed. M. Lewis and J. M. Haviland-Jones (New York: Gilford Press, 2000), 637–53, which summarizes the research and gives extensive references to it. My discussion in *Hiding from Humanity* cites other more detailed studies, and related work by other psychologists.

21. Some of these feelings may involve skepticism about whether danger has really been removed; others may be triggered by memories—e.g. of the cockroach being dropped into the juice. Some of these cases of disgust

could be defended as, broadly, rational. Still, such arguments do not rehabilitate the emotion as generally reliable.

22. Rozin never explicitly makes this point; I add it in *Hiding from Humanity* in defending his basic argument.

23. See Erving Goffman, *Stigma: Notes on the Management of Spoiled Identity* (New York: Simon and Schuster, 1963).

24. See the perceptive analysis in William Ian Miller, *The Anatomy of Disgust* (Cambridge, MA: Harvard University Press, 1997), 109–42.

25. Weininger, *Sex and Character*, English translation based on sixth German edition (London: W. Heinemann, 1906), 300. (Weininger, a self-hating Jew and homosexual, committed suicide in 1903.)

26. Yoel Inbar (Harvard University), David Pizzaro (Cornell Univesrity), Joshua Knobe (UNC–Chapel Hill), and Paul Bloom (Yale University), "Disgust Sensitivity Predicts Intuitive Disapporoval of Gays," *Emotion* 9 (2009), 435–39.

27. If we articulated this reason, however, we would have to admit that many policies we now tolerate toward other animals cause harms similar to those we forbid in the case of dogs: here again, disgust prevents us from asking pertinent questions.

28. See the longer treatment in *Hiding from Humanity*.

29. *Dalit* is the appropriate way to refer to the people who were formerly called "untouchable."

30. Why don't *dalits* change their names? Name changing in India is difficult and cumbersome, requiring both time and publicity. Upper castes will mock the *dalit* for a name change, and lower castes will criticize such a person severely for lack of solidarity.

31. The last name is the key way in which one recognizes caste, and the only reliable way. The first two names are *dalit* names, the names, in fact, of two prominent *dalit* politicians: Nehru's law minister was B. R. Ambedkar, a *dalit* who converted to Buddhism; the current head of the University Grants Commission, Sukhadeo Thorat, is the *dalit* son of a

sharecropper, who has publicly described being shunned and stigmatized by other children during his childhood (despite the fact that he is roughly coeval with the Indian constitution). The other two names are easily recognizable in India as Bengali Brahmin names.

32. See Dover, *Greek Homosexuality*.

33. Poland, by contrast, still has a great deal of intense antigay feeling, as does Russia.

34. This difference was already remarked on by Freud after he taught in the United States. He suggested that Americans had channeled their libido into moneymaking rather than giving it a sophisticated adult development. See Henry Abelove, "Freud, Male Homosexuality, and the Americans," *Dissent* 33 (1985–86), 59–69.

CHAPTER TWO

The Politics of Humanity:
Religion, Race, Gender, Disability

The feelings were not passing as they were supposed to. They were staying and I was beginning to get scared. At first, the label was very negative. This was when I was fifteen years old. I tried to engage in behavior that would encourage heterosexuality, such as looking at girls, imagining their breasts, and trying to date them. I read my bible six times that one year to find a way out of my predicament. My senior year I gave up outgrowing it.

I was reading sort of all this educational stuff about homosexuality and it portrayed it in a positive way and that is, that they have their own culture and their own heroes and models. So at this point then I was able to say to myself that I am gay myself.

—TWO INTERVIEWEES IN RITCH SAVIN-WILLIAMS,
"...AND THEN I BECAME GAY"

We hold these truths to be self-evident, that all men are created equal, that they are endowed by their Creator with certain unalienable rights, that among these are life, liberty and the pursuit of happiness.

U.S. *Declaration of Independence*

I. RESPECT FOR PERSONS, SPHERES OF LIBERTY

What is the politics of humanity? Centrally, it is a politics of equal respect. Our nation is built on the idea that all citizens as citizens are of equal worth and dignity. Rejecting the feudalism and monarchism of their European experience, our forefathers rejected all titles, ranks, and hereditary honors. A person's birth, wealth, and status had no bearing on his political opportunities and entitlements. The American Revolution was in that sense radical, rejecting all previous modes of social organization and opting for one entirely new, built on the idea that all persons have equal human dignity and equal natural rights.[1] The key idea of the new political order came to be one of nondomination: the idea that what was centrally bad, in politics, was the systematic subordination of some citizens to others.[2] Because all citizens are equal, domination, whether based on class or religion or some other principle, must be firmly rejected.

The Founders were famously obtuse on some matters. While articulating the general principle of nondomination, they allowed slavery, permitting race to be a ground of brutal domination—even though slavery, and the slave trade, had already been firmly rejected by most of Europe. They also failed to respect the equal humanity of Native Americans. Nor did their ruminations about the equality of "men" extend to women, despite the fact that partisans of equal natural rights in France and England had already challenged this ground of domination.

Nevertheless, the general principle the Founders articulated has held firm over the years, providing a basis for challenges to its originally narrow application. Thus Abraham Lincoln, in the Gettysburg Address, could allude without hypocrisy to the promise of liberty and equality in the Declaration of Independence as a moral basis for the war effort. And thus, one hundred years later, Martin Luther King Jr. could also allude to the Declaration of Independence as

> a promissory note to which every American was to fall heir. This note was a promise that all men, yes, black men as well as white men, would be guaranteed the "inalienable Rights" of "Life, Liberty and the pursuit of Happiness." It is obvious today that America has defaulted on this promissory note, insofar as her citizens of color are concerned.[3]

And thus women could similarly challenge their exclusion from political equality by invoking the promise of America's founding documents that all who share in humanity would share, as well, in equality. Susan B. Anthony, in her famous speech on the right to vote, alluded to the preamble to the Constitution when she said:

> It was we, the people; not we, the white male citizens; nor yet we, the male citizens; but we, the whole people, who formed the Union. And we formed it, not to give the blessings of liberty, but to secure them; not to the half of ourselves and the half of our posterity, but to the whole people—women as well as men. And it is a downright mockery to talk to women of their enjoyment of the blessings of liberty while they are denied the use of the only means of securing them provided by this democratic-republican government—the ballot. [4]

Our founding documents, then, are properly construed as more egalitarian in their general promise of human equality than in the particular understanding of that equality that was prevalent at the time of their composition.

These founding documents, and the idea of nondomination that lies at their heart, say nothing about being a nice or even a moral person. Equal natural rights belong to us all as our birthright, not because we are virtuous or because we conform to particular social norms. Just as a person's distinguished parentage or property ownership does not confer a title to greater political rights, so too a person's moral virtue does not give that person more votes than a stingy, or ill-tempered, or silly, or cowardly, or self-indulgent, or unfair person has.

If a political right is fundamental, then, it may not be abridged because the majority judges that a person is not very nice, or behaves badly. All individuals, of course, are equally subject to the criminal law, and if they violate it their rights may be for a time abridged. (We shall face later the question how far it is permissible for the criminal law to enforce controversial moral judgments, or to penalize people for conduct that does not harm others.) As people and citizens, however, all start in a position of fundamental equality, with equal political entitlements. Respecting one's fellow citizens as equals doesn't mean approving of their choices, but it does mean respecting their right to make certain choices consistent with the principles of equal dignity and equal entitlement.

The Declaration of Independence speaks of a right to the "pursuit of happiness" as among the inalienable rights of all persons. While this language is not in the Constitution, the Constitution recognizes such an entitlement in many concrete ways, including in its promise (as the preamble states) to "secure the blessings of liberty to ourselves and our posterity." In general, the Constitution recognizes that equal respect for individuals requires the protection of extensive spheres of liberty, so that they may engage in conduct that is meaningful and significant, forming a key part, for them, of the pursuit of happiness (speech, religious belief and practice, etc.). This liberty is not given only to nice people, just as it is not given only to rich people. It is given equally to all.

Gays and lesbians have never been denied the right to vote, and have never been enslaved. On the other hand, they have sometimes been denied the equal right to vote (Colorado's Amendment 2 denied them the right to pass local laws protecting themselves from discrimination in employment, housing, etc.), and they have certainly been denied the right to the equal pursuit of happiness. Heterosexuals are generally free to pursue sexual fulfillment in a wide variety of ways, whether they are selfish or decent, frivolous or capable of commitment. Before *Lawrence v. Texas*, by contrast, gays and lesbians in many states could be sent to prison for pursuing sexual fulfillment in their own characteristic ways.[5] Marriage, often deemed a "fundamental right," has been and still is unavailable to same-sex couples in most states.

This chapter will argue that the promise of equal liberty inherent in our constitutional tradition supports the radical rethinking of the politics of sexual orientation that we have been conducting over the past twenty years. Equal respect for the human dignity and natural rights of all persons, as a fundamental American value, entails many specific criticisms of legal treatments of sexual orientation, just as this fundamental value earlier entailed a rethinking of issues of religion, race, and gender. As we think about what a politics of equal respect requires, it is useful to consider those earlier rethinkings. Drawing on the legal tradition in areas in which the ideas of equal respect and equal liberty have been more thoroughly pondered will help us deliberate about what equal respect requires in the area of sexual orientation.

Thinking through these comparisons will not remove our need to wrestle with constitutional text and tradition. That task awaits us in later chapters. It will, however, suggest general directions of thought about fundamental constitutional values. Such thoughts can orient us in a helpful way. It's sometimes good to move away from a controversial topic for a while, in order to revisit it after reflecting on possible analogies.

2. SEARCHING FOR THE MEANING OF LIFE AND SELF: SEXUAL ORIENTATION AND RELIGION

Many of the first American colonists came to the New World in search of religious freedom. Dissenters of many types from the Anglican orthodoxy of Britain—Catholics, Baptists, Calvinists, Quakers, and many others—they sought both the freedom to express their beliefs without penalty and the freedom to practice their chosen forms of worship. Often, they failed to connect their search to politics of respect and toleration inclusive of those who disagreed with them. Thus, many of the colonies established a state church, inflicting disadvantages, whether severe (imprisonment, banishment) or subtle (being taxed for the support of the dominant church), upon religious minorities.

Gradually, however, the very experience of living—often in taxing physical conditions—with people whose religious convictions differed from their own led many colonists to the realization that a good common life, and perhaps survival itself, required protecting religious liberty for all, and doing so with an even hand. Such policies had practical sources: people needed one another's help if they were going to flourish in the new land. They also began to notice that people who differed from them in religious conviction could be helpful and upright as fellow citizens. They began to notice that it was possible to live together on the basis of a moral consensus about values such as fairness, honesty, and impartiality, without necessarily agreeing on theological first principles. In tolerant colonies such as Rhode Island and Pennsylvania, people of widely varying beliefs and practices managed to live together peaceably on terms of mutual respect. Rhode Island, for example, welcomed not only a range of Puritan dissenters, but also Baptists, Quakers, Roman Catholics, Jews, and (officially at least) Muslims, and also established good relations with the native inhabitants, on the basis of a fair-minded agreement to respect their property rights. Roger Williams, the colony's founder, even insisted on including atheists in the new group as citizens with rights and privileges equal to those of others.[6]

The trend in favor of religious liberty emerged, then, from the very experience of living together. It also had a theoretical foundation, in the idea of *conscience* that many if not most of the new settlers brought with them. This idea, in its original form, is Protestant, though heavily influenced by the Roman Stoic philosophy that was so important to many of the colonists.[7] We can find similar ideas today in most of the world's major religions and in the thought of many secular people. According to this view, all human beings have a capacity for searching for life's ultimate significance and moral basis—for the meaning of life, we might say. This capacity is a key part of what constitutes our dignity as human beings. Conscience is present in all human beings, regardless of their beliefs, and it is present equally. Indeed, it is the major source of our equality, and this equality must be recognized, and respected, by any decent political order. Conscience often goes astray: indeed most of the time it does. But the fact that someone goes astray does not imply that this person does not have the power of conscience in equal measure with others. It is this capacity that we ought to respect, not this or that mode of its exercise, and that means giving equal respect to all human beings.

The early settlers were very far from having a view that many if not most Americans now have—namely, that many, or even all, religions are legitimate paths to salvation. Virtually none of the early colonists accepted such a view. They all thought that many of their fellow citizens were damned. Nor did they respect those people's beliefs and practices. They did not say, "Probably they are damned, but their practices are good efforts and deserve our support and respect." Roger Williams, for example, refers to Native American religion as "satanic"—even while consistently showing the most delicate respect and friendship to its practitioners. We should not delude ourselves into thinking, then, that the policies of religious respect and fairness that gradually came to dominate in the colonies, shaping our Constitution, were inspired by respect for differing religious beliefs and practices. Rather, they were inspired by a more basic underlying idea of respect for persons, for our fellow citizens as bearers of human dignity and conscience. Even when we believe others are going astray, the faculty of conscience in them deserves respect from our laws and institutions. Because human beings are of equal worth, conscience is deserving of equal respect.

We might treat people with equal respect by giving none of them any significant liberty. The American tradition, however, argues that respecting conscience involves granting ample liberty to each person to pursue his or her own way in matters of conscience. Roger Williams used two illuminating metaphors. Conscience, he said, must not be imprisoned—meaning that people must be given plenty of space to practice their religions, including acts of worship that their conscience dictates. Even more abhorrent than imprisonment was what Williams memorably called "Soule rape"—the violation of a person's very inner world by the demand for professions of faith that go against the promptings of conscience. A world that respects conscience therefore gives equal liberty to all people to pursue its promptings in matters concerning both belief and conduct.

The settlers understood that people can be forced to convert. They had seen this all the time. And even if compulsion didn't work in the first generation, they knew that over time it would gradually homogenize a population. They knew that religion is a human choice and not an immutable characteristic. But the fact that religion is not immutable did not mean to most settlers that it was permissible to force religious change upon people. Respect for conscience stood in the way: we do not have a right to compel people in their search for the ultimate meaning of life.

As the colonists experimented with different forms of political order, they gradually embraced another conclusion that Roger Williams drew from his insight about equal liberty: a world of equal respect for conscience cannot have an established state church, even a benign one that does not threaten or imprison. The chief architect of early American thought about establishment, James Madison—whose ideas continue to be highly influential in our tradition of constitutional interpretation—insisted that the establishment of an official state church threatens the equality of citizens by making a statement that some forms of religion are "ours," while others are merely tolerated—thus setting up a hierarchy among citizens.[8] Equal respect for conscience means a vigilant refusal to countenance the participation of government in any creation of in-groups and out-groups, especially in the realm of religion.

Now let's think about sex. Very few Americans today think that sexual happiness is a trivial matter. For many if not most people, it is a central part of one's search for the meaning of life. Even if sex is in many ways unlike religion, it is like it in being intimately personal, connected to a sense of life's ultimate significance, and utterly nontrivial. Like religion, it appears to be something in which authenticity, or the involvement of conscience, is central. We understand that it goes to the heart of people's self-definition, their search for identity and self-expression.

If we follow the parallel, we arrive at a picture of life in which people, respecting one another's human dignity, conclude that it is wrong to demand of all citizens one particular mode of sexual conduct. There should be plenty of liberty to believe what one likes about sex and to express those beliefs in action—with limits set, as in the religion case, by the protection of the legitimate interests of others. As with religion in the early days of the republic, so with sex today: many people view the practices of some of their fellow citizens with profound aversion. But they ought to respect the practitioners as their equals; respecting them as their equals, they should conclude that it is wrong to deny them the chance to search for meaning in their own way.

Now of course the pursuit of sexual happiness is in many important ways unlike religion. Many people will feel that the very comparison is offensive. I do not intend to say that the values involved are the same, or even of the same magnitude. Nonetheless, the point of the analogy is to say that the pursuit of sexual happiness is viewed by most Americans as a very intimate and important part of the pursuit of happiness, a part that touches on the core of the self. Nor is this a mere majority fad: we can give good reasons for thinking sexual expression bound up with the core of a person's identity and personality, and with the most intimate aspects of striving and searching for meaning. For that reason, one might argue, it is important for people to be able to manage the choices involved in their sexual lives themselves, without interference from the state, unless they violate the rights of others. That thought, as we shall see, is a major part of our unfolding constitutional tradition in this area. (If we follow the parallel to the free exercise clause, we will want not just some liberty, but liberty that is given on equal conditions to all.)

That is the "free exercise" side of the analogy. But what about the establishment side? Could the state give everyone plenty of sexual liberty and still announce that a particular style of sexual interaction is preferred, and support that preference with public policies of various sorts, in ways that go beyond the state's legitimate interest in protecting the welfare of children? The religion analogy at least suggests that the answer should be "no." For the state even to "establish" a particular sexual style as the privileged one is to imply the inferiority of those not practicing the preferred style.

That side of our analogy is at issue today in the heated debate over same-sex marriage. Unlike the liberty side, concerning which we have arrived at a wide consensus, the idea of nonestablishment, in sexual matters, does not command a consensus either in public life or in the law.

Religion is a good analogy to think with, because it reminds us that we may think other people wrong and sinful in matters of the deepest moral importance while yet agreeing that respect for them as equal citizens requires according them a broad sphere of liberty of both thought and conduct. It also implies that we should not establish an orthodoxy that ranks some citizens above others.

3. SYSTEMATIC DISADVANTAGE: SEXUAL ORIENTATION
AND RACE, GENDER, DISABILITY

Our nation has struggled with the idea of equality throughout its history, gradually putting an end to the systematic subordination of African-Americans and of women—at least in the law—and beginning to protect the equality of people with disabilities. Our unfolding constitutional understanding of what equal protection of the laws means, in the areas of race, gender, and disability, gives us not only general illumination, as the religion analogy did, but also legally pertinent arguments that we can apply to the case of sexual orientation.

On one understanding of the Equal Protection Clause of the Fourteenth Amendment, influential in an earlier era, what is required is formally similar treatment. If group A is treated in the same way as group B, no equal protection problem is raised. Segregated schools were often defended in this way: as "separate but equal" facilities, which therefore raised no equality problem. In *Brown v. Board of Education*,[9] however, the Supreme Court unequivocally rejected that interpretation. Insisting on segregation's effect on self-esteem and human development, the Court wrote that segregation "generates a feeling of inferiority as to [minority children's] status in the community that may affect their hearts and minds in a way unlikely ever to be undone." That asymmetry of human opportunity was masked by the appearance of formally similar treatment. Equal protection forbids a majority to give a minority systematic disadvantages that, in effect, ensure their subordination—even if the policy at issue is apparently neutral.

Similarly, and significantly for constitutional questions involving sexual orientation, when laws against miscegenation were challenged in the 1960s, they were defended, once again, by appeal to their formal symmetry: blacks couldn't marry whites, and whites couldn't marry blacks.[10] The state of Virginia argued that in light of this symmetry miscegenation laws "do not constitute an invidious discrimination based upon race."[11] The Supreme Court, however, looked beneath the formal symmetry, asking about the meaning of the prohibition on miscegenation for people's substantive equality, their opportunities, their overall social standing. The prohibition, they concluded, was not truly symmetrical, because it was part of the enforcement of white supremacy: it carried a stigma that made the rights of blacks systematically unequal, and was a type of "invidious racial discrimination." Equal protection, the Court holds, requires more than formally similar treatment: crucially, it requires nonsubordination.

An equally resonant equal protection case, in the area of gender, is *United States v. Virginia*, which opened the doors of the Virginia Military Institute (VMI) to women.[12] Once again, there was an appearance of formal equality, because Virginia provided an alternative program for women at Mary Baldwin College. The Court, however, inquired in detail into the opportunities opened to students by each of these programs, concluding that, to be constitutionally satisfactory, the state's substitute program must place women in "the position they would have occupied in the absence of [discrimination].'" Because the Mary Baldwin program was merely a "pale shadow" of VMI, the situation constituted an unconstitutional discrimination based upon sex.

Equal protection, thus understood, captures an idea of nonsubordination that stretches back to the nation's founding.[13] The law shows truly equal respect for citizens only if it looks searchingly into apparent symmetries, examining the real opportunities different groups of citizens have to pursue what is important in life. (This idea of equal protection, once deeply entrenched in the reasoning of the Court, is now weaker; in the area of race-based remedies, it seems to have become a minority position.)

Without delving prematurely into the concrete constitutional issues that need to be faced in applying the Equal Protection Clause to the case of sexual orientation, we can already see that there is an important analogy between the cases of race and gender and that case. In all three areas, history reveals that some ways of classifying people are particularly likely to embody prejudice and to cement hierarchies that compromise the equality of citizens. Later we will need to unpack this analogy further, identifying the criteria that link sexual orientation to race and gender in ways that are different from other characteristics (such as being a smoker, or liking to drive fast). Already, however, we can see that in all three cases—race, gender, and sexual orientation—we are dealing with deep-seated characteristics of people that pervade their lives and that have frequently been the source of stigma and subordination. Surely, the idea of nonsubordination has promise for thinking about sexual orientation.

Thus, a prohibition that targets sex acts performed by homosexuals, while leaving unrestricted similar sex acts performed by heterosexuals, appears to create the same type of equal protection problem that was created by laws against sex between blacks and whites. Many people also believe that laws prohibiting same-sex marriage, while allowing opposite-sex marriage, are similar to laws against interracial marriage; as we shall see, courts have sometimes held this, although the analogy remains controversial. More generally, the case of sexual orientation seems analogous to gender and race because, in all three cases, people are being classified by a trait, and then being denied fundamental opportunities in a wide range of areas because of that trait.

As in the case of religion, the rejection of systematic disadvantages for a group does not require the majority to like the group in question, or to think that what they believe or do is good. Misogynists and racists can support the legal regime inaugurated by *Brown*, *Loving*, and the gender cases—just as people who believe that members of other religious groups are "satanic" can support equal religious liberty—just so long as they hold the basic view that all citizens are and ought to be equal under the law. Indeed, it is difficult to see how a person who holds that basic American idea can reject the antisubordination regime defined by cases such as *Brown* and *Loving*—unless that person is so preoccupied with ideas of contamination and stigma (which were a large part of the segregationist ideal and, even more, of the laws against miscegenation) that he or she cannot even focus clearly on the meaning of the equality ideal.

Because the idea of rooting out systematic disadvantage is so central to the purpose of the Equal Protection Clause, the interpretive tradition has recognized that heightened scrutiny is warranted whenever legal rules deal with certain classifications that are particularly likely to be linked to hierarchy and discrimination: in other words, these classifications must be supported by an unusually strong justification. Called *suspect classifications*, these ways of categorizing people have to pass not mere rational basis review, which is not a very demanding standard (almost anything that a legislature thinks a good reason is allowed to count as a rational basis), but, instead, a more searching test. Thus, legal classifications involving race can only be justified if the state can show that the use of race is necessary to achieve a compelling state interest. Classifications involving gender are examined with an intermediate standard of scrutiny, and are sometimes called *quasi-suspect* classifications.

We shall later discuss the criteria for heightened scrutiny in considerable detail, because it is much debated whether sexual orientation is a suspect classification, and, if so, on what basis. Without entering into that legal discussion, however, we can already see that the general spirit of the idea of heightened scrutiny is pertinent to thinking about sodomy laws, same-sex marriage, and other related questions. Certain ways of categorizing people embody a legacy of hierarchy and therefore cannot be permitted to stand, under the Equal Protection Clause, unless a very important state interest requires the restriction.

There is one further group whose equality we need to consider, because it will later prove useful in thinking about equal protection law in the area of sexual orientation. This is the (highly heterogeneous) group of people with disabilities. These people, like members of racial minorities and women, have long been denied fully equal legal rights in American society, and that denial has often been fueled by irrational fear and prejudice. In two cases involving exclusion of children with disabilities from the public schools, courts have held that the exclusion was an equal protection violation. *Mills v. Board of Education* even cited *Brown* as a precedent, arguing that the systematic, legally enforced refusal to educate children with physical and mental disabilities alongside others was a basic denial of their equality before the law.[14] The case did not discuss the issue of heightened scrutiny, but the court did say that the increase in cost to government involved in educating children with disabilities is not a sufficiently strong state interest to make the policy of exclusion legal.

At around the same time, the Supreme Court found that an exclusionary zoning ordinance passed by a Texas city violated the Equal Protection Clause, failing even to pass rational basis review. *City of Cleburne v. Cleburne Living Center*[15] invalidated the denial of a permit for a group home for people with mental retardation. (Permits were not required for convalescent homes, homes for the elderly, and sanatoriums, not to mention boardinghouses, fraternity and sorority houses, dormitories, hospitals, and hotels: only for "homes for the insane or feeble-minded or alcoholics or drug addicts.") The denial of the permit was plainly prompted by fear and other negative attitudes expressed by nearby property owners.

Disability has never been recognized as a "suspect classification," and *Cleburne* explicitly denied that it was one.[16] Interestingly, however, the Court found that the much less taxing standard of rational basis review, according to which a law must be "rationally related to a legitimate governmental purpose," was violated by the zoning ordinance. "The short of it is," the Court declared, "that requiring the permit in this case appears to us to rest on an irrational prejudice against the mentally retarded."[17] The city council, the Court concluded, passed the ordinance in deference to the "negative attitude" of property owners. "But mere negative attitudes, or fear, unsubstantiated by factors which are properly cognizable in a zoning proceeding, are not permissible bases for treating a home for the mentally retarded differently from apartment houses, multiple dwellings, and the like."[18] Significantly, the Court emphasized that the mere fact that a law reflects the will of a democratic majority is not sufficient to avoid the strictures of the Equal Protection Clause.

"It is plain that the electorate as a whole, whether by referendum or otherwise, could not order city action violative of the Equal Protection Clause."[19] The Court held that the Equal Protection Clause prohibits laws based only on dislike or disgust, even if a majority wants them—a conclusion that the Court had anticipated in *Department of Agriculture v. Moreno*,[20] a case concerning requirements in a federal food stamps program that discriminated against nontraditional families. As we'll see, *Cleburne* and *Moreno* are important precedents for one of the landmark Supreme Court cases involving sexual orientation, *Romer v. Evans*.

4. THE NEED FOR IMAGINATION

What we have seen emerging in these different areas of constitutional law is a legal understanding based on a more fundamental idea of equality. However, equality and equal respect cannot come into being, or long survive, without the ability to imagine the situation of a person in a different social group and to assess it from that person's point of view. To the Puritans of Massachusetts, worshippers in other faiths looked like witches or demons, Satan's agents in our midst. The fact that these other people were seeking in good faith to find the meaning of life was difficult to see because of the Puritans' hatred of the path these people had chosen. Other settlers soon saw or began to see things differently: though the practices of others (whether Jews or Baptists or Native Americans) might still be rejected as sinful and bad, the people were increasingly approached in a spirit of imagination and understanding. From that point of view, they seemed relevantly similar. "I am seeking for meaning in a very mysterious world; you are doing that too. I think I am right and you are wrong, but we are both seekers, both following the faculty of conscience that is the proper focus of our respect for one another." Roger Williams addresses his great work on religious equality to "the merciful and compassionate reader," knowing that the ability to see the other not as an agent of Satan, but as a person like oneself, struggling with difficult problems in a confusing world, was essential for the politics of religious respect that he was outlining. (Notice that this approach is perfectly compatible with holding, as Williams did, that the religious *practices* of the Native Americans were satanic.)

A politics of disgust and fear used to dominate in religious matters. People shrank from (allegedly) defiling contact with Satan's apostles. To people who approach others with disgust, you cannot simply say, "Respect this other person." Such people are not ready for respect, because they cannot really, or fully, see the person as a person. Disgust diminishes the other, making "those" people look base, more like animals or devils,[21] without the full dignity of a person. Respect for conscience requires, at the very least, the ability to see that the other is a person, with a conscience and pursuing a conscientious search. That ability to imagine what the other person is pursuing and that it is indeed a person (not a monster) pursuing it, is an indispensable step on the way to the thoughts about equal liberty that have become central to our American tradition.

Before we can attain a politics of respect in matters of sexual orientation, people have to be able to imagine what gays and lesbians are pursuing, and see it as relevantly similar to their own search for personal and sexual integrity and expression. They still may not approve of what these other people are doing: they still may think gays and lesbians sinful, or misguided, or disobedient to the word of God. But the crucial first step toward respect will have been taken.

Significantly, this ability to imagine what the other is pursuing has played a key part in the modern understanding of equal protection. Separate but equal facilities (whether for gender or for race) can seem fair enough, on paper. What tells us that such facilities do not show equal respect? In *Brown*, it required a patient effort to imagine the obstacles faced by children in the allegedly equal black schools. Only this exercise of historically and socially informed imagining showed that these schools were not really equal, that the stigma surrounding segregation imposed asymmetrical harms.

In *Loving*, one might have thought that empathy would come easy: after all, what these people wanted was to get married, and that seems like a pretty easy thing to understand as a human purpose, and to relate to one's own concerns. Nonetheless, that was not the way racists saw miscegenation. They did not see a man and a woman seeking a life of committed happiness, but something disgusting and defiling, something from which their senses literally shrank. Instead of the pursuit of happiness, corruption of the blood; instead of passion and commitment, nefarious and dirty predation. For judges to get to the point at which they could say that the laws against interracial marriage were a mere expression of white supremacy, they had to move beyond that way of thinking, and they had to see the similarity of the aims of Mildred Jeter and Richard Loving to the aims of people who seek to marry within their race.

Similarly, in *U.S. v. Virginia*, women's legitimate interest in high-level education and employment opportunities must be understood before the substitute program at Mary Baldwin College looks inadequate. For many centuries, women were shunted into finishing schools instead of colleges and universities, and this did not look like an unequal state of affairs. To see the inequality, one must first see the person, and see the person not just as a convenient object for the service of men, but as an equal fellow citizen, trying to achieve a variety of purposes in American society. Respect for women requires and rests upon the ability to see how their purposes are similar to those of men; and this requires imagination.[22]

The idea that constitutional adjudication requires imagination does not turn the law into a soft morality of "*tout comprendre, c'est tout pardonner.*" Indeed, notice that imagination was exercised, in the cases I have discussed, on both sides of the matter. Judges had to identify the purpose animating the antimiscegenation laws, and that required them to see into the ideas of contamination and taint that constituted "white supremacy," before they could articulate what that legal regime was all about. In *Cleburne*, even more clearly, the attitude of the Texas majority had to be considered to determine whether it reflected rational argument or just fear and irrational loathing. That sort of scrutiny, too, is a way of showing respect to one's fellow citizens: we expect them to have a rational purpose for the laws that they pass, and if they do not have one, then we do not allow even a democratic majority to use the law as an instrument to inflict disadvantages on others.

The combination of equal respect for one's fellow citizens with a serious and sympathetic attempt to imagine what interests they are pursuing is what I have called the politics of humanity. I have suggested here that the sort of imagining I describe is crucial, perhaps even necessary, as a precursor to respect. But we should now go further, asking whether it isn't more intimately related to respect, a part of what respect itself involves. To respect another person as an equal is to see that person in a certain way: as an end, not merely as a means, as a person, not merely as an object. That way of seeing requires endowing the other with life and purpose, rather than with dirt and dross, with human dignity rather than with foulness. This idea that respect involves an effort of imagination is not just a liberal idea. Indeed, it has been eloquently developed in a recent book by Charles Fried, who was Ronald Reagan's Solicitor General. Fried notes that many straight people think that the sex lives of gays and lesbians are strange. In that sense, asking them to imagine those lives may seem like asking people to imagine a color they have never seen. But, continues Fried,

Some such effort is morally required of us if we are to respect the humanity and liberty of gay people. The alternative is to deny their humanity, which would be hideous, for we are talking of thinking, feeling human beings who are literally our brothers and sisters. That effort—and it is a possible one—is to acknowledge simply that gay people have sexual longings just like straight people do and that those longings occupy an analogous place in the geography of their spirits. That imaginative effort is, after all, perhaps only a step beyond a man's empathy for the sexual desires of a woman, and that empathy is a perfection of sexual love.[23]

In essence, the demand is at the heart of ideas of morality that animate many if not most of the world's great religions, as well as many of its secular moralities: the idea that we must learn to see, and love, our neighbor as ourselves. Put that way, the demand is both new and old, both time-honored and profoundly radical.[24]

As I've said, the politics of humanity doesn't connote approval of the choices other people make, or even respect for the actions they perform. It just requires seeing them as human beings of equal dignity and equal entitlement pursuing a wide range of human purposes. In some cases those purposes may involve real harm to others. In such cases, we may legitimately restrict people's ability to pursue them. But the person who practices the politics of humanity never retreats to a position from which the equal humanity of others can't be seen.

Such, I shall now argue, has been the vantage point from which an earlier legal regime saw the sexual life of gays and lesbians. Between *Bowers v. Hardwick* and *Lawrence v. Texas*, a crucial shift took place in our nation's constitutional thinking; it was enabled by a shift in the imagination.

NOTES

1. See Gordon Wood, *The Radicalism of the American Revolution* (New York: Vintage, 1991). For the debt of many American thinkers to Roman republicanism, see Wood, *Radicalism of the American Revolution*, and my *Liberty of Conscience: In Defense of America's Tradition of Religious Equality* (New York: Basic Books, 2007), chap. 3.

2. See Philip Pettit, *Republicanism: A Theory of Freedom and Government* (New York: Oxford University Press, 1997).

3. Martin Luther King, Jr., "I Have a Dream," August 28, 1963, https://www.americanrhetoric.com/speeches/mlkihaveadream.

4. Susan B. Anthony, "On Women's Right to Vote," (1873), http://www.historyplace.com/speeches/anthony.htm.

5. As we shall see, sodomy laws were often worded neutrally, prohibiting certain acts by both heterosexuals and homosexuals. They were, however, typically enforced only against homosexuals. Moreover, they left homosexuals few legal ways of pursuing sexual satisfaction, while heterosexuals had ample options.

6. On Williams, see Nussbaum, *Liberty of Conscience*, chap. 2.

7. For the influence of Stoicism on the Founders, see Wood, *Radicalism of the American Revolution*, and Nussbaum, *Liberty of Conscience*, chaps. 2 and 3.

8. For discussion of Madison's *Memorial and Remonstrance*, see Nussbaum, *Liberty of Conscience*, chaps. 3 and 6.

9. *Brown v. Board of Education of Topeka*, 347 U.S. 483 (1954).

10. *Loving v. Commonwealth of Virginia*, 388 U.S. 1 (1967).

11. Cited in the majority opinion of *Loving*.

12. *United States v. Virginia*, 518 U.S. 515 (1996).

13. See Pettit, *Republicanism*.

14. 348 F. Supp. 866 (D. DC 1972).

15. 473 U.S. 432 (1985).

16. Actually, the Court denied that it was a quasi-suspect classification (as is gender), deserving "intermediate" scrutiny—as the Fifth Circuit had found.

17. 473 U.S. 450 (1985).

18. Ibid., 448.

19. Ibid.

20. 413 U.S. 528 (1973), see chapter 4.

21. It is not surprising that the devil is often represented in the form of animals that inspire disgust, such as bats or insects.

22. These themes are more fully developed in my "Foreword: Constitutions and Capabilities: 'Perception' against Lofty Formalism" (*Harvard Law Review* 121 [2007], 5–97), together with discussion of some striking failures of imagination in the 2007 Supreme Court term, in the areas of both gender and race.

23. Charles Fried, *Modern Liberty* (New York: Norton, 2007), 140. Note, however, that Fried has not entirely shaken off an older politics of disgust: for he immediately tells his reader that "such an effort of imagination forces the straight person to abstract from the physical details of gay sex and move to a more general idea of sex."

24. Isn't there a type of disgust that functions as the ally of this sort of sympathetic imagining, for example disgust at intolerant and prejudiced people? This is a long and complicated question, which I treat at length in *Hiding from Humanity: Disgust, Shame, and the Law* (Princeton: Princeton University Press, 2004), chap. 2. Briefly: (a) In many such cases the word *disgust* is used loosely, and the emotion in question is really anger, an emotion linked to the ideas of harm and rectification. (b) When it is not used loosely, disgust is not a socially useful emotion; it tells us to avoid contact with the bad people, to stigmatize them, not to respect them as equals, while it tells us that we ourselves are pure and free from fault. Both of these messages are a very bad basis for political life in a nation of equals who disagree.

[53]

CHAPTER THREE

Sodomy Laws: Disgust and Intrusion

Although the meaning of the principle that "all men are created equal" is not always clear, it surely must mean that every free citizen has the same interest in "liberty" that the members of the majority share. From the standpoint of the individual, the homosexual and the heterosexual have the same interest in deciding how he will live his own life, and, more narrowly, how he will conduct himself in his personal and voluntary associations with his companions. State intrusion into the private conduct of either is equally burdensome.

—JUSTICE STEVENS,
DISSENTING OPINION IN *BOWERS V. HARDWICK*

I asked [Officer] Torick if he would leave the room so we could get dressed and he said, "There's no reason for that, because I have already seen you in your most intimate aspect."

—MICHAEL HARDWICK,
DESCRIBING HIS ARREST IN HIS OWN BEDROOM[1]

I. TWO VISIONS OF SOCIETY: DEVLIN VERSUS MILL

Sodomy laws are intrusive. Under the laws that used to exist in all states, what people did consensually and in seclusion, without inflicting anything on outsiders, without even the knowledge of outsiders, could become the basis for criminal prosecution and, often, for severe criminal punishment. Public enforcement of personal sexual conduct was once the norm in both Britain and the United States. To most Americans today, however, it seems outrageous that the police would have the right to enter someone's bedroom to see what sexual acts are being performed there. Officer Torick's response to Michael Hardwick's polite request (as he stood in Hardwick's bedroom after serving a warrant for public possession of alcohol that had expired ten days before) conjures up, for most of us, the specter of a police state, and we know we don't want to go there.

It's not just the loss of liberty that makes Officer Torick's remark scary, it's something deeper: an insult to human dignity reminiscent of prisons and even concentration camps, where the removal of simple bodily privacy became a way of marking some people as not fully human.

Despite the fact that most Americans would probably react with disapproval to such intrusive behavior by an officer of the law, the road to a decisive rejection of such governmental scrutiny and coercive control of consensual intimate conduct, in our constitutional tradition, was long and difficult. Michael Hardwick died in 1991, before he could see the vindication of his right to intimate association.

Legal regulation of sexual conduct raises profound questions about the type of society we want to be. Lord Patrick Devlin preferred a picture of society in which the key value is solidarity. Personal liberty counts for something, Devlin concedes, but it can always be trumped by sufficiently strong feelings of disgust and abhorrence on the part of the majority. That's the basic idea animating the politics of disgust.

Devlin aimed his arguments, above all, against the very different conception of society favored by nineteenth-century British philosopher John Stuart Mill. Mill lived in an England even more intrusive and puritanical than yesterday's America. As a young man, he went to jail for distributing information about contraception in the slums of London. For a long stretch of his adult life, he was treated as a social pariah by many for his intimate friendship with Harriet Taylor, a married woman—despite the fact that her husband did not object, and the pair almost certainly did not have sexual relations until after the husband's death and their own marriage. On the basis of this and other experiences, Mill came to abhor the tyranny of public sentiment over personal choice. In his famous work *On Liberty*, he argued that conduct that involves only the interests of those who participate in it (he called this "self-regarding" conduct) is never a proper object of legal regulation. Gambling, drinking, unusual sexual behavior—all these might be morally objectionable to most people, but they could not properly be regulated so long as they involve only those who choose to perform them. Conduct is appropriate for legal regulation, Mill argued, only when it is "other-regarding," when it interferes with nonconsenting others.

Behind Mill's distinction is a deep idea about people: that they need zones of freedom around them in order to work out their own course in life, and that these zones of freedom ought to protect, above all, certain rights of personal decision and association. A society that protects these zones of liberty, Mill believed, will be both more just to individuals and stronger as a whole than a society that allows conventional norms to tyrannize over personal freedom. It is just this idea that we have been investigating in thinking about the analogy between religion and sexual expression.

To see what is at issue between Devlin and Mill, we need to distinguish three different ways in which sexual conduct might potentially affect the interests of others. First, it might involve some type of violence or coercion. Both Devlin and Mill agree that such conduct (for example, rape or child abuse) is properly regulated by law.[2]

Second, it might involve the infliction of a direct offense that is comparable to a harm or a rights violation. We can understand this category most easily by thinking of the legal category of nuisance: disgusting smells or sounds on my neighbor's property that spoil my enjoyment of my own give me a cause of legal action. Here we can see that rights are being directly violated by the nuisance, in a way that looks very close to battery or assault.[3] Notice that this sort of offense, insofar as disgust is involved, concerns the primary objects of disgust, not projective disgust.

Offense is very difficult to think well about when we move beyond such simple cases of noise or odor, but it looks as if at least some sexual behavior is in this category. If someone masturbates on a public bus, or exposes himself in the public street, this seems, at least, to be nuisance-like, and we feel that it is not simply self-regarding in Mill's sense. (In many such cases, furthermore, we know that the person's aim is often to inflict the conduct on unwilling spectators: exhibitionism involves an intention to shock and disturb.) Our judgment that this type of conduct is not self-regarding is perhaps clearest when it affects children, but it's at least plausible to think that the direct offense to adults is also a harm in a way that is close to harms in the first category. The case is clearest where primary objects of disgust are involved: thus, public defecation, which involves unpleasant smells and possible health issues, is a clearer case of direct offense than is public nudity, where any disgust people feel seems to be mediated by social ideas. Mill does not clearly discuss such cases, but it's pretty clear that they do not lie within the zone of liberty that he is striving to protect.

In dealing with what I have called direct offense in the law, we should be sensitive to constrained circumstances and to the nature of the actors. Thus, a toddler who defecates on a public playground should not be legally penalized, but an adult who defecates on that same playground could be. In designing and enforcing laws against offensive behavior, we need to allow public disgust (at primary objects) to play some role, but we need to be acutely sensitive to constrained circumstances. Thus, a homeless person who urinates in a railway station should be treated with greater leniency than a stockbroker who does the same thing. The issue is not just economic: a distance runner who defecates in an alleyway during a marathon, even if a stockbroker, should not be treated the same way as that same person would be treated if he or she were to defecate in a public building after lunch.[4]

In regulating direct offense, we should insist that the disgust in question involves primary objects in some way: thus, disgust at the public display of affection by an interracial or same-sex couple does not constitute a legally regulable harm in this sense, because the disgust is projective, not oriented to primary objects (bodily fluids, odors, etc.). The very idea that direct offense is legally regulable rests on an idea that the object is causing a sort of harm, and this idea cannot be defended without alluding to the role of primary objects.

Finally, there are cases where the conduct is consensual and takes place in seclusion, not impinging directly on any third party, but where other people are upset when they imagine that it is going on. This is what Mill called a "merely constructive" injury: people imagine how offended they would be if they were present at those acts, and in the process of imagining that, they get all worked up and feel disgust and indignation. Notice that, insofar as disgust is involved in such cases, it is always projective: no primary objects are present, and typically one's fantasy is not even really focused upon them, but, rather, upon some alleged link between them and the person whose acts one is contemplating. (Thus, people usually don't get all worked up thinking about people defecating or urinating in their own bathrooms; instead, they get worked up thinking about the sex acts of people whom, in fantasy, they link to feces and other disgust-objects.) Many types of consensual conduct in seclusion arouse strong emotions in other people when they imagine them going on. In addition to same-sex sexual acts, adultery, fornication, and masturbation (all once objects of legal regulation and some of them still so in many states), we could mention nude dancing in private clubs, nudity on private beaches, consensual sex acts in private sex clubs, and—to move from the sexual to other related cases—the possession and consumption of alcohol in seclusion, gambling in seclusion or in a private club, and so on. Many laws regulating such "self-regarding" conduct remain on the books. As recently as 1991, the Supreme Court upheld an Indiana law forbidding nude dancing in private clubs, arguing that considerations of public morality made such laws constitutionally acceptable—overruling a passionate opinion from the Seventh Circuit Court of Appeals that held that the dancing was expression protected by the First Amendment.[5]

The debate between Devlin and Mill concerns this last group of cases. For Devlin, the "constructive" disgust of the average member of society is sufficient reason to regulate "self-regarding" conduct by law, even though the actions in question cause neither harm nor direct, nuisance-like offense. For Mill, such zones of seclusion and personal liberty are definitive of a free and healthy society.

What is involved, as we shift from a politics of disgust to a politics of humanity, is that more general question about the sort of society we wish to have. In essence, it is the age-old debate between proponents of collectivism and proponents of important spheres of individual liberty. This is not a left-right issue. Many Marxist movements have been as intrusive in sexual matters as the most vehement religious conservatives. In the 1970s, leftist movements on campuses prescribed what correct sexual behavior was for men and women, what clothes good men and women should wear, when one should get married and when one should not, and so on. They were disagreeing with the conservatives they opposed only over what should be regulated, not over the propriety of intrusive regulation. In the "middle," but it wasn't really a middle, sat the uncomfortable Millian, dismayed by the cavalier way in which both sides treated individual liberty.

The question we must ask, then, is not whether we like the left better than the right or the right better than the left. To portray this issue as one that pits the academic left against ordinary conservative folks is profoundly misleading.[6] The question, instead, is whether, at the most basic level of our political organization, we believe that the fundamental political unit, the primary bearer of entitlements, is the person or the group. Does the individual have certain zones of freedom, certain rights, that cannot be taken away by the judgments of a collectivity, or does the collective interest always trump individual entitlement?

In the area of religion, America, far more than Europe, has consistently sided against collectivist values and in favor of a strong respect for the individual's zone of liberty. Most Americans are surprised and dismayed, for example, at the laws forbidding the Muslim headscarf or the Jewish yarmulke in certain parts of the public sphere (public schools, government employment) that are now common in many parts of Europe.[7] In sexual matters, however, America and Britain have, on the whole, been more sympathetic than continental Europe to the collectivist position, favoring a good deal of public supervision of "morals," whereas continental Europe has been more protective of the individual. (All laws against consensual adult sexual activity were abolished in France, for example, early in the twentieth century—at a time when anal intercourse, whether heterosexual or homosexual, was still a capital offense in Britain.[8]) Americans have been deeply attached to liberty of conscience, but we haven't until much more recently been able to see sexual choices as issues of conscience, choices for the individuals involved, alone, to make.

Despite our distinctive history, however, the time seems to have come when we can all agree that some intimately personal matters are simply not matters for the police to control—or even to watch.

2. HISTORY: SODOMY LAWS IN THEORY AND PRACTICE

Sodomy laws are very old. They are part of the Anglo-American legal tradition, and at one time they were recognized, in some form, by every state in the United States. Until 1961, all fifty states outlawed sodomy under some description. At the time of *Bowers v. Hardwick* (1986), twenty-four states still had such laws.

Sodomy laws have had two distinct purposes. One has been the regulation of nonprocreative sexual acts, for heterosexuals as well as homosexuals: above all, anal and oral sex acts, although some statutes include mutual masturbation and penetration by a physical object. Here are a few samples of laws, unrestricted as to the gender of the parties, that were on the books at the time of *Bowers v. Hardwick*:

Maryland: Sodomy is a felony. Taking another person's sexual organ into one's mouth or placing one's sexual organ into another person's mouth, or committing any other unnatural or perverted sexual practice with any other person, is also a felony. In an indictment under this section, it is not necessary to set forth the particular manner in which such unnatural or perverted sexual practice was committed.

[61]

Florida: Whoever commits an unnatural and lascivious act with another person is guilty of a misdemeanor. A mother's breast feeding of her baby does not violate this section.

Oklahoma: It is a felony to commit the detestable and abominable crime against nature. Any sexual penetration, however slight, is sufficient to complete the crime against nature.

Arizona: A person who knowingly and without force commits, in any unnatural manner, any lewd or lascivious act upon or with the body or any part or member thereof of a male or female adult, with the intent of arousing, appealing to, or gratifying the lust, passion, or sexual desires of either of such persons, is guilty of a misdemeanor.

Also of interest for its long laundry list of forbidden acts, though the context makes it clear that it is limited to same-sex actors, is this law from Missouri:

Deviate sexual intercourse means any act involving the genitals of one person and the mouth, tongue, or anus of another person, or a sexual act involving the penetration, however, slight, of the male or female sex organs by a finger, instrument, or object done for the purpose of arousing or gratifying the sexual desire of any person.

Such laws are as striking for their vagueness as for their intrusiveness. Presumably legislators wanted to avoid what they took to be offensive language; they also wanted to avoid giving people ideas. The result is a high degree of unclarity about what is forbidden. Officers of the law are allowed enormous latitude in construing such phrases as "lascivious," "unnatural," and the ubiquitous "any other." Maryland's statute even encourages vagueness in the indictment itself. Missouri's unusually clear law explicitly criminalizes use of a finger in the vagina or anus, as well as the use of any object for the purpose of sexual stimulation of another: but other statutes, including many of the sex-neutral ones, probably intend to include such conduct under the vague catchall rubric "any other." The extent of the laws' vagueness is marked by the striking Florida law, which feels the need to warn officers of the law against arresting breast-feeding mothers for an "unnatural sexual practice." If that was envisaged by legislators as a possible construal of the general language of the statute, one can see how vague it is.

Sodomy laws, then, though later targeted at homosexual acts, are originally a form of highly intrusive and highly general regulation of sexual practices in which millions of Americans engage. Similarly, the crime of "buggery" under British law, although limited to anal intercourse, included such intercourse between a man and a woman as well as between two men. Like the American laws, these early sodomy laws were clearly aimed at policing nonprocreative sexual relations, although in the nature of things they were enforced against married couples.[9]

A second purpose of such laws, which seems to have developed in Britain and, to a lesser extent, elsewhere in Europe late in the nineteenth century, and which is reflected in a minority of U.S. statutes at the time of *Bowers*, is the policing of homosexual acts in particular. British law seems never to have worried about lesbians, and their likely sex acts were never illegal.[10] (Nor was Britain worried about oral sex or the use of objects between heterosexuals or between women.) For males, however, the offense of sodomy (the more modern name for "buggery") was thought not to sweep widely enough—although sodomy, a capital crime until 1861, remained punishable by a prison term of from ten years to life. A new law, which would criminalize a much broader group of homosexual acts, was proposed by Henry Labouchère and passed by Parliament in 1885, as an amendment to a popular bill designed to protect women against trafficking by raising the age of consent from thirteen to sixteen. The Labouchère Amendment provided that "[a]ny male person who, in public or in private, commits...any act of gross indecency with another male person, shall be guilty of a misdemeanor, and being convicted thereof, shall be liable...to be imprisoned for any term not exceeding two years with or without hard labor."[11]

By this time, legislators appeared not to be very worried about anal intercourse between men and women (although the distribution of contraceptives and contraceptive information remained a crime long after, the crime for which John Stuart Mill went to jail as a young man); and the British never worried about lesbians. A veritable hysteria about male homosexuality, however, led to numerous arrests and convictions, including the famous conviction of Oscar Wilde. Wilde had foolishly brought a libel action against the Marquess of Queensberry, who had left a note at Wilde's club saying that Wilde was "posing as a sodomite" (only he could not spell the word, and wrote "somdomite"). After Queensberry won the libel action on grounds of justification, Wilde was prosecuted—under the Labouchère Amendment, not the sodomy law, because Wilde preferred oral sex, and there was no evidence that he had ever had anal intercourse with any of his contacts. A first trial ended in a hung jury, but the second led to a conviction and the maximum prison sentence. Wilde's health was broken, and he died in France at the age of forty-six.

Wilde's sentencing provides a typical example of the politics of disgust. Mr. Justice Wills said:

> Oscar Wilde and Alfred Taylor, the crime of which you have been convicted is so bad that one has to put stern restraint upon one's self to prevent one's self from describing, in language which I would rather not use, the sentiments which must rise to the breast of every man of honour who has heard the details of

these two terrible trials.... It is no use for me to address you. People who can do these things must be dead to all sense of shame, and one cannot hope to produce any effect upon them. It is the worst case I have ever tried.

This is Devlin country, and though the justice chose not to describe his "sentiments," his violent repudiation of the defendants made his disgust amply evident. Indeed, we might say that his whole speech (which was much longer than this) is more like vomiting than like judicial argument. This judge had been on the bench for some time, dealing with homicides, rapes, and many other serious offenses. What had Wilde done to merit the label "worst case"? He had had oral sex with a sequence of male prostitutes (only one nonprostitute, and this one was in his twenties and sought out Wilde eagerly, so there is no issue of "corruption of the young"). He treated all his partners with the utmost kindness and generosity, giving them expensive gifts—items, such as engraved silver cigarette cases, that later helped to convict him. The sex took place in seclusion, usually in posh hotels, so there was no issue of direct offense to onlookers. It seems simple lunacy to call this a "worst case." And yet that was the way in which Victorian Britain as a whole regarded it—not without enormous hypocrisy, since male-male sex acts, as well as sadistic beatings, were the staple of life in elite male "public schools."

With heterosexual sodomy in Britain, then, we have stern policing, followed by gradual desuetude—but no violent public disgust. With homosexual acts, the politics of disgust carried the day and was not challenged until the Wolfenden Commission report in 1957 (the occasion for Devlin's famous defense of disgust).

Things were much the same in the United States: most early statutes criminalized a wide range of sexual acts, originally, it would appear, policing a wide and somewhat indeterminate range of nonreproductive acts. As time went on, however, zealots focused obsessively on the policing of (especially male) homosexuality. The U.S. laws sweep far more broadly than the British laws ever did. Virtually all of them include oral and anal acts together; typically, they apply to lesbians as well as to heterosexuals and homosexual men; and many of them include a very wide range of common heterosexual acts. Some are so vague that they might be construed as applying to solitary masturbation (Arizona's, for example, doesn't require "another person," but only "a male or female adult"). Nonetheless, the likelihood that a solitary person or a married couple would be prosecuted under such laws was always slight, and even unmarried heterosexual couples would be prosecuted under them, typically, only as an extra offense added to a charge of adultery or fornication. As time went on and even the adultery and fornications laws fell into desuetude, the moralists' zeal focused intently, and increasingly, as in Britain, on same-sex acts—above all those performed by males.

The reasons for this shift are not altogether easy to discern. Victorian morality, like its American counterpart, was strict in all kinds of ways, and its special anxiety about same-sex acts between men is a little difficult to understand today. I can remember from my childhood the special disgusted shrinking with which the topic of male homosexuality was mentioned, at a time when oral sex between heterosexuals would have been no big deal; but, as with disgust generally, the reasons for this asymmetry, in Britain as in the United States, are hard to discern. Perhaps, however, it was the sheer dominance and prominence of men that gave rise to anxiety lest their sexuality express itself in nonreproductive and nonpatriarchal ways. (This interpretation finds support in the unusual zeal with which society went after men such as Wilde, who chose to lead openly "deviant" lives.[12]) And although continental Europe was less persecutory in many ways, Germany followed the trend, criminalizing same-sex acts between men for the first time in 1871.[13] (As in Britain, such acts between women were never illegal.)

Sodomy laws raise three distinct problems. First, they are intolerably, even absurdly, intrusive. What business does the state have telling me where I should put my finger, or, more generally, what acts I may perform with a willing partner? Most Americans today reject even the laws against adultery, although in that case a Millian could argue that a contract affecting the interests of the spouse is being violated. (Breach of contract, however, is a civil, not a criminal offense.) Certainly by now most Americans reject state policing of all consensual sexual behavior, and for a very long time they have rejected it where heterosexuals are concerned. Second, many of the laws are intolerably vague, leaving far too much to the discretion of the interpreting agents of government. Vagueness typically raises constitutional problems. Third, the statutes are either discriminatory on their face, criminalizing only the acts of homosexuals and leaving similar acts performed by heterosexuals untouched, or else they are discriminatory in application, enforced, in recent times at least, only against homosexuals. We might add that their intrusiveness is worse for homosexuals than for heterosexuals, because the prudent heterosexual can figure out a way to be a law-abiding citizen without giving up sex altogether, while the homosexual basically has to give up sexual relationships completely (although mutual masturbation is still allowed by most statutes, unless it is covered by expressions such as "any other unnatural or perverted sexual practice").

Sodomy laws had a demonstrable connection to violence against lesbians and, particularly, gay men. By defining gay men as outlaws, they gave notice to people prone to violence that violence against that group was not going to be taken as seriously as violence against other citizens. Gary David Comstock, in his important study of antigay violence, concluded that the typical perpetrator in a

[67]

gay-bashing incident was not someone with a deep-seated hatred of homosexuals. It was, instead, someone (often young and drunk) eager for a fight, who believed, plausibly, that the police would look the other way if a gay man were the victim.[14] Indeed, as his study showed, police were often themselves perpetrators. One anonymous policeman from a large city said that he had beaten up seventeen gay men during the past year alone. Officer Torick's zealous pursuit of Michael Hardwick, and his glee at being able to place Hardwick in an undignified and humiliating position, are not idiosyncratic. Nor is the beating that Hardwick subsequently received at the hands of three men who drove up to his house, tore all the cartilage out of his nose, kicked him in the face, and cracked about six of his ribs.[15] What provoked the assault? The public knowledge that Hardwick had been charged with public drinking at a known gay bar, which identified him as a homosexual and (hence) an outlaw. In this case and in many others, sodomy laws have a lot to answer for.

3. LIBERTY, PRIVACY, AND THE FOURTEENTH AMENDMENT

The Constitution's Fourteenth Amendment states (in part): "No State shall make or enforce any law which shall abridge the privileges or immunities of citizens of the United States; nor shall any State deprive any person of life, liberty, or property, without due process of law; nor deny to any person within its jurisdiction the equal protection of the laws." Added shortly after the Civil War, the amendment was aimed above all at ensuring that the southern states could not withdraw basic rights from the former slaves. Over the years, the amendment has become a pivotal device for protection of all individuals' fundamental entitlements, but particularly those of persons from marginalized or subordinated groups. Although at times during this history the "privileges and immunities" clause has played an important role in this struggle, for our purposes the relevant clauses are the second and third, the Due Process and Equal Protection clauses. Thinking about these clauses and what they protect is complicated and more than a little confusing, since both clauses have been seen to protect fundamental liberties, and both also have a strong equality component.

As we saw in chapter 2, the Equal Protection Clause protects subordinated groups from laws that embody or further systematic hierarchy and subordination. In some cases, we saw, it has also protected citizens not in one of those recognized groups from a basic violation of their equal entitlements motivated by animus or fear. There is, however, another aspect to equal protection, because it has been that clause through which certain fundamental rights of citizens not enumerated in the Constitution—the right to vote, for example, and the right to travel—have been recognized and given constitutional standing. This aspect of equal protection will concern us no further in the present chapter, but it will become important in the following one, because *Romer v. Evans*, a major case involving the protection of gays and lesbians against discrimination, was initially argued with reference to that equal protection tradition.

For now, however, let us focus on the way in which substantive personal liberties have been protected through the Due Process Clause. There can be no doubt that the Due Process Clause protects citizens from procedural violations of their rights. What has been far more controversial is the question whether the clause protects substantive liberties. "Substantive due process" got a bad reputation during the Progressive Era, when justices hostile to legislation protecting workers used the clause to strike down a variety of progressive reforms, including minimum wage and maximum hours laws, on the ground that they interfered with the "liberty of contract." For many years after that, there was considerable reluctance to use the clause to protect substantive liberties—until growing discontent with intrusive sexual regulation made the Court take a new look at that possibility.

The modern revival of substantive due process was triggered by a Connecticut law that made it a crime to use "any drug or article" to prevent conception and also, in a separate "accessory" statute, criminalized contraceptive counseling and the provision of contraceptive advice. The director of Planned Parenthood and its medical director had been convicted and fined under the accessory statute for giving advice on contraception and prescribing contraceptive devices, for married couples. (Thus the law was challenged only as it limited the rights of married people.) In 1965, the Supreme Court held that the law violated the Due Process Clause of the Fourteenth Amendment.[16] Famously, the opinion by Justice Douglas recognized a "right to privacy," arguing that this right, though not specifically mentioned in the text of the Constitution, was implicit in the "penumbras" and "emanations" of other rights (such as the Fourth Amendment right to be free from unwarranted search and seizure).

Griswold v. Connecticut concerned an unenumerated right that might seem progressive, part of a movement toward "sexual liberation." (Of course, married couples had long used various means of artificial contraception, and the advent of the pill only made its use easier for both married and unmarried people.) The reasoning in the case, however, has nothing to do with "liberal" preferences. Suppose we imagine a law, like that once in force in China, that prohibited married couples from having more than one child: this law would be invalidated as unconstitutional under *Griswold*, and for similar reasons. As I've argued, the threat to the dignity and autonomy of the individual comes from both the right and the left, and *Griswold* stands for the idea that the person has basic rights to nonintrusion, even though these are not all enumerated.

Griswold has become the basis for a series of highly controversial "right to privacy" cases, prominently including *Roe v. Wade*,[17] which protected a (limited) abortion right. As often happens with controversy, key issues have become muddied, and it is sometimes suggested that the very fact that a right is not explicitly enumerated in the Constitution means that illicit politics is involved in its recognition. People believe this, however, only because they have been encouraged to consider the privacy right in isolation, rather than to look at the many ways in which unenumerated rights have been recognized. In fact, nobody should be surprised to find that the Constitution protects rights that are not enumerated in it. Some of our most cherished rights (the right to vote, the right to travel) have this status (being recognized as implicit in the Equal Protection Clause). Even the most conservative jurists do not contest these unenumerated rights. Nor, in fact, does any suggest that the Due Process Clause does not protect liberty rights that need further specification and definition. The opposition does not sweep this broadly: it confines itself to attacking the privacy right as itself illegitimate. I do not believe that the opposition has given good reasons why this right is not a legitimate one for judges to recognize, while the other long-familiar ones are.

The basic project in which Justice Douglas was engaging is not only not illicit, it is central to our constitutional tradition. Nonetheless, as a legal theory, Justice Douglas's account of "penumbras" has struck many scholars as murky. Many have also found the very concept of privacy unclear, and in certain ways misleading, and I shall agree with them. It is important, however, to distinguish two different questions: Does the Due Process Clause provide a basis for recognizing unenumerated liberty rights in the area of sexual choice? And: should we approve of the particular way in which Justice Douglas argued this?

The answer to the first question is "yes." Just as our tradition has recognized as implicit in the Equal Protection Clause certain unenumerated rights on which we rely every day, so too, our long-standing tradition has affirmed that the Due Process Clause protects some unenumerated rights in the area of "liberty." Liberty, after all, is explicitly mentioned in the text, so what judges are doing is working out, as they must, what that term covers. This is the inevitable task of judicial interpretation, when the Constitution gives judges only a highly general notion, such as "the free exercise of religion," or, in this case, "liberty."

James Madison, chief architect of our constitution, was well aware that enumeration of certain rights in a Bill of Rights might be construed to deny the constitutional significance of other rights not so enumerated, and for this reason he proposed the Ninth Amendment, which states that "the enumeration in the Constitution, of certain rights, shall not be construed to deny or disparage others retained by the people."

Such unenumerated liberty rights had repeatedly been found in the Due Process Clause well before the controversial postulation of a "right to privacy." In 1923, in *Meyer v. Nebraska*,[18] the Court invalidated a law that made it a crime to teach any modern language other than English in a public or private school. The Court recognized a broad range of liberty rights as implicit in the Due Process Clause:

> Not merely freedom from bodily restraint but also the right of the individual to contract, to engage in any of the common occupations of life, to acquire useful knowledge, to marry, establish a home and bring up children, to worship God according to the dictates of his own conscience, and generally to enjoy those privileges long recognized at common law as essential to the orderly pursuit of happiness.

Two years later, in *Pierce v. Society of Sisters*,[19] the Court invalidated a law requiring all children to attend public, rather than private, schools, because it unconstitutionally interfered with the "liberty of parents and guardians to direct the upbringing and education of children under their control." This set of cases was summarized by Justice Brandeis in 1928, in a formulation that, although initially set out in a dissenting opinion, has again and again been cited as definitive of a long liberty tradition:

> The makers of our Constitution undertook to secure conditions favorable to the pursuit of happiness. They recognized the significance of man's spiritual nature, of his feelings and of his intellect. They knew that only a part of the pain, pleasure and satisfactions of life are to be found in material things. They sought to protect Americans in their beliefs, their thoughts, their emotions and their sensations. They conferred, as against the Government, the right to be let alone—the most comprehensive of rights and the right most valued by civilized men.[20]

So the Due Process Clause has been understood to protect some rights in the general area of intimate association, including, but not limited to, rights involving the family. *Griswold* correctly relied on this line of cases in order to protect the use of contraception by married couples in the home.

Are these liberty rights limited to married couples? In 1972, in *Eisenstadt v. Baird*,[21] the Court said that they were not. *Eisenstadt* concerned the distribution of contraceptive foam to unmarried women at a public meeting. It was argued under the Equal Protection Clause, not the Due Process Clause, but its conclusion is important for the understanding of due process liberty: "[W]hatever the rights of the individual to access to contraceptives may be, the rights must be the same for the unmarried and the married alike...since the constitutionally protected right of privacy inheres in the individual, not the marital couple." Rightly seeing that the Fourteenth

Amendment ascribes rights to the "person," not to groups or collectivities, not even to couples, *Eisenstadt* reasoned that the liberty rights found in *Griswold* and other related cases are individual rights of persons to make certain intimate choices for themselves. Once we see them that way, the Equal Protection Clause requires us (the Court held) to extend those rights to the unmarried.

> [T]he marital couple is not an independent entity with a mind and heart of its own, but an association of two individuals each with a separate intellectual and emotional makeup. If the right of privacy means anything, it is the right of the individual, married or single, to be free from unwarranted governmental intrusion into matters so fundamentally affecting a person as the decision whether to bear or beget a child.

What should be clear, then, is that there is a long tradition of recognizing, under the Due Process Clause, a set of liberty interests in the area of intimate association. Some of these pertain to marriage and the family, but even those are understood to be decisional rights of individuals, and *Eisenstadt* explicitly stated that rights relating to sexual choice belong to unmarried as well as married individuals.

Griswold was right to invalidate the intrusive Connecticut law on due process grounds. But there is plenty of room to find fault with the way in which Justice Douglas argued, and especially with the notion of privacy that he invoked. Privacy is one of the most vague and confusing concepts in the law.[22] It includes ideas of informational secrecy, modesty, seclusion, and decisional autonomy, in a potentially confusing way. In the area of sexual liberty, the idea of privacy suggests an idea of decisional freedom, the idea that certain choices (of intimate association, of childbearing and contraception) are for people to make on their own, with no supervision from the state. It also suggests an idea of seclusion, pertinent to the protection of others from offense, and the idea of the home as privileged space, where government has no business. In *Griswold*, for example, Justice Douglas asks rhetorically, "Would we allow the police to search the sacred precincts of marital bedrooms for telltale signs of the use of contraceptives?"

The decisional component of privacy and the idea of the home as a protected place are not unrelated. They are connected through the idea of seclusion. If we return to the three categories of sexual behavior we distinguished earlier, we can see that it is plausible to believe that the decisions that are a person's own to make, those that should not be controlled by the state, are only those in our third category—decisions that involve only those who consent and not others who might be harmed by the choice. Acts that take place in seclusion, if fully consensual, are usually free from harm to nonconsenting parties. The home is one example of a place of seclusion—though far from the only example. If acts are performed in the home, and are fully consensual, then they are usually self-regarding in Mill's sense. Acts done in a public place are more likely to involve the interests of nonconsenting parties. But the Millian idea of self-regarding conduct is not equivalent to the idea of the home as a privileged space. Many actions in the home are not consensual and harm nonconsenting parties. The appeal to the (alleged) privacy of the home has all too frequently been used to protect child abuse, domestic violence, and marital rape from the law's scrutiny. Moreover, conduct may be self-regarding in Mill's sense even when it occurs outside the home: for it might take place in a hotel room, or a private club, or even a secluded outdoor spot.

What is unfortunate about *Griswold* and the line of cases descending from it is not, then, that it recognizes substantive liberty rights in the area of intimate association as implicit in the Due Process Clause, but the way *Griswold* and subsequent cases mix the decisional aspect of privacy with the spatial aspect, suggesting that the domain of the home is a privileged place of decisional liberty, a kind of government-free zone.

A case that makes this move particularly clearly is *Stanley v. Georgia*,[23] in which the Court held that a person has a right to the private use of obscenity—in the home. The Court might have held that the personal possession and use of obscenity in seclusion, without direct offense to others, is protected by the Constitution. Instead, the Court muddied the waters by speaking of a "right to satisfy his intellectual and emotional needs in the privacy of his own home," and by concluding that the states' power to regulate obscenity "does not extend to mere possession by the individual in the privacy of his own home." Had Stanley been reading his magazines in a hotel room, or in a cabin temporarily rented for a vacation, what then? Are the police authorized to search resorts, hotels, offices in a private place of business for evidence of possession of obscene materials? And why would those secluded places be deserving of less protection than the home? The Court's appeal to "the home" is resonant rhetorically, but not very helpful analytically.[24]

One more source of potential confusion must now be cleared away. The Due Process Clause has often been thought to be traditional, or backward looking, because two influential formulations describe the liberties protected by the clause as those that are "deeply rooted in this Nation's history and tradition"[25] and "implicit in the concept of ordered liberty."[26] Even if tradition were our only guideposts, however, there is still a genus-species problem: for, while it might be true that the right of homosexuals to engage in homosexual sodomy does not, as such, fit those descriptions, at a more general level our tradition does recognize a right of persons to choose to make intimate decisions about their sexual lives—most clearly for the married, but *Eisenstadt* extends that right to the unmarried. Furthermore, there are other formulations of due process that suggest a less tradition-based approach: for example, one formulation insists that the inquiry should be whether a right "is of such a character that it cannot be denied without violating those fundamental principles of liberty and justice which lie at the base of all our civil and political institutions."[27] A right of intimate association, crafted so as to exclude acts that harm nonconsenting parties, meets this specification.

4. *BOWERS V. HARDWICK:* INTRUSION AND OBTUSENESS

Michael Hardwick, a gay man, was drinking a beer after work, in a gay bar where he had been helping friends install some insulation.[28] As he prepared to leave, he tossed the beer into the trash can by the front door of the bar. At this very moment, a police car drove by. Seeing Hardwick, the officer drove back and asked Hardwick where the beer was. Hardwick said he had thrown it into the trash. The officer made Hardwick get into the police car and asked what he had been doing at that bar. Hardwick said that he worked there, which identified him as a homosexual. The policeman asked Hardwick to show him the bottle that he said he had thrown into the trash, but the contents of the trash can could not be seen from the car, and Hardwick was afraid to get out of the car without explicit authorization. Eventually the policeman gave Hardwick a ticket for drinking in public, but the ticket was filled out erroneously, with two different court dates on two different parts of the ticket. When Hardwick didn't show up for the earlier one (because the later one was at the top of the ticket), a warrant was issued for his arrest. Two hours later, Officer Torick arrived at Hardwick's house. Usually it takes forty-eight hours to process a warrant, but Torick processed it personally, taking a zealous interest in the case.

When Torick arrived, Hardwick was not at home, but when Hardwick heard from a roommate that an officer had been there with a warrant, he went downtown and showed the two dates on the ticket to the clerk, who fined him $50, which he paid. The clerk gave him a receipt and expressed surprise that Torick had personally processed the warrant. Three weeks later, Hardwick was beaten up by three young men in front of his house: word of his orientation had evidently spread.

Several days later, Officer Torick arrived at Hardwick's house. A visiting friend of Hardwick's, sleeping on the couch, answered the door. (By this time the warrant had been invalid for more than three weeks.) Torick came to the bedroom and opened the door. Hardwick remembers hearing a noise, but then thinking that it was just the wind. He went back to what he was doing, which was mutual oral sex with a male partner. Almost a minute went by before Officer Torick made his presence known and announced that Hardwick was under arrest. "I said, For what? What are you doing in my bedroom?" Torick said he had a warrant. Hardwick pointed out that the warrant was no longer valid. Torick said it didn't matter because he had been acting in good faith. After refusing to leave while Hardwick and his friend got dressed, he took them to the station house, told all the other prisoners that they were homosexuals (actually, he told guards and other prison officials that Hardwick was there for "cocksucking" and that he should be able to get plenty of that in prison). Hardwick was booked for sodomy. The Georgia law, enacted in 1816, said that "a person commits the offense of sodomy when he performs or submits to any sexual act involving the sex organs of one person and the mouth or anus of another."

At this point, the American Civil Liberties Union took an interest in Hardwick's case and decided that it provided a good opportunity to challenge the sodomy law, since the sex was between two consenting adults and took place in seclusion. For a time, a heterosexual couple, the "Does," joined the challenge to Georgia's sodomy law, which was orientation neutral, but they were denied standing by the district court because they faced no "immediate danger of sustaining some direct injury as a result of the statute's enforcement." Thus the state admitted that the statute, though neutral, was unequally enforced.

The state's strategy was to focus relentlessly on homosexual conduct rather than on the broader notion of forbidden sex acts. When the case was argued before the Supreme Court, Georgia Attorney General Bowers kept referring to homosexuality throughout his argument, and claimed in his brief that "homosexual sodomy leads to other deviate practices such as sadomasochism, group orgies, or transvestism, to name only a few." (Hardwick had never been associated with any of these practices.) Bowers repeatedly alluded to "gay baths" and suggested a link between the sodomy law and the state's interest in public health. Although Paul Cameron's most outrageous claims were not foregrounded, the state's general strategy was the Cameron strategy of disgust and fear—despite the fact that both the American Psychological Association and the American Public Health Association had emphasized the frequency of the outlawed practices among heterosexuals, including eighty percent of married couples. Harvard law professor Lawrence Tribe, arguing the case for Hardwick, attempted to get the Court to focus on the general issue of intrusiveness and the limits of government power, emphasizing the secluded and intimate nature of Hardwick's sexual activity in a way that argued for a more general human interest in noninterference.

On June 30, 1986, the Supreme Court upheld the sodomy law by a 5–4 vote. (The result later became even more controversial when it was divulged that Justice Powell had changed his vote at the last minute—only to regret his position later on and publicly admit that he had probably been wrong.[29]) The crucial defect of the majority opinion (by Justice White) and the even harsher concurring opinion by Chief Justice Burger is a deficiency of human imagination—of "humanity" in the sense I have given that term.

Why, one might ask, do judges need to use their imaginations? Surely their job is to interpret the Constitution faithfully. Yes, to be sure—but this case, like many difficult cases that reach the Supreme Court, cannot be resolved by any purely technical argument. Instead, judges have to consider relevant similarities and differences, and this means that they have to try to understand human aims and interests. In order to determine whether the rights curtailed by the Georgia sodomy law are protected by the Due Process Clause, a judge must first figure out the relevant specification of those rights. Does this law threaten a right of all persons to consensual intimate association? So described, the right looks like one that is both fundamental and deep, and this description of what is at stake is naturally suggested by the text of the Georgia law, which applies to persons of all sexual orientations. To see whether that description of the right is pertinent, a judge would have to ask whether the liberty claimed by Michael Hardwick is relevantly similar to the decisional rights of individuals already recognized by the Court.

Justice White, however, considered the issue narrowly, as "whether the Federal Constitution confers a fundamental right upon homosexuals to engage in sodomy." He then says that it is "evident that none of the rights announced in those [earlier privacy] cases bears any resemblance to the claimed constitutional right of homosexuals to engage in acts of sodomy." To claim Due Process Clause protection for such a right "is, at best, facetious." Similarly, Chief Justice Burger, in a harsh concurring opinion, opines that "the proscriptions against sodomy have very 'ancient roots,'" concluding: "To hold that the act of homosexual sodomy is somehow protected as a fundamental right would be to cast aside millennia of moral teaching."

These judgments get some things badly wrong on the facts. As we've seen, the special zeal to restrict homosexual activity under the sodomy laws is of rather recent origin. Nor does the entire "history of Western civilization" show opprobrium directed at these acts. Same-sex acts between women have hardly ever been prohibited, and were not so even in England. Heterosexual "sodomy" was an approved practice in many ancient societies, including ancient Greece, where, as I've noted, anal sex often served contraceptive purposes. (In many societies, anal sex also served to preserve female virginity.) Same-sex relations between men were carefully scrutinized in Greece because of widespread disapproval of a citizen's playing a passive role, but some acts prohibited under later sodomy laws were publicly approved, and many more such acts were widely tolerated. Erotic attraction between men was regarded as normal and natural, and even the gods were imagined as having such love affairs. To move to modern times, all criminal penalties for consensual sexual acts were abolished in France by the early nineteenth century. Such historical and international facts may or may not be relevant to the judgments of a U.S. court, but because they were invoked, it is important to point out that they were invoked incorrectly.

History, however, is hardly the primary problem. These two opinions are morally obtuse in a way that shocks. Even at the time, when widespread animus and prejudice against homosexuals still existed in the United States, it should have been easy to see that what they were asking to be able to do legally bore not "no resemblance," but a very close resemblance to what heterosexuals often do legally. It had already been established by *Eisenstadt* that the rights associated with sexual intimacy are individual rights, and rights of the unmarried as well as the married; so the Court could not defend its obtuseness by saying that marriage is the only relationship that the Fourteenth Amendment protects. The ability to make decisions concerning one's sexuality had been held to be a fundamental individual right, and it doesn't take a leap of creativity, but only a rather ordinary step of imagination, to see that this was what Michael Hardwick was seeking. What he was doing in his bedroom was exactly like what millions of heterosexuals, married and unmarried, were doing legally all over America.

How could someone in good faith conclude that that there was "no resemblance" between the rights invoked in his case and those recognized in others? We need, here, to think, again, about the politics of disgust: the way in which homosexuals were routinely portrayed as somehow not fully human, as something like the cockroach that crawls onto your kitchen floor. You sort of know it is there, but you don't want to admit it is there, so you don't look at it very hard. Years of stigmatization of gays and lesbians made it all too easy for judges, unaware that some of their friends and relations were gay and lesbian, to talk about them as a class of moral pariahs who are not like other humans. Bowers's oral argument strongly supported that way of thinking. The abhorrence expressed by the majority opinion and by Burger's concurrence inhabits the same world as Justice Wills's condemnation of Oscar Wilde, and shows the same unwillingness to try to see, from the point of view of the homosexual person, what is being sought and what its resemblance is to the actions and rights of heterosexuals.

Reinforcing the harshness of these opinions is their Devlinesque character: they allude to long-standing traditions as if those, by themselves, settle the matter of what rights individuals have under the Constitution. As we've seen, the appeal to disgust and a solidaristic conception of society are very closely linked in Devlin: it is the value of solidarity that makes the appeal to disgust legally relevant. These two opinions don't theorize in that way, but they do rationalize their stigmatizing by reference to tradition. As the dissenting opinion points out, however, the rights recognized in earlier cases were not (Devlinesque) rights of cohesive social collectivities; they were decisional rights of individuals involving intimate association and the personal pursuit of happiness. Such rights do not cease to exist simply because a majority doesn't like them. The Court, however, could not see that Michael Hardwick was pursuing happiness like other people, because they focused on the unpopular and (allegedly) nontraditional category of "homosexual sodomy." The two sides in *Bowers* thus replay the Devlin-Mill debate, showing us clearly what is at stake in the choice between the two conceptions of society.

The dissenting opinion by Justice Blackmun makes interesting use of the religion analogy, arguing that a "necessary corollary of giving individuals freedom to choose how to conduct their lives is acceptance of the fact that different individuals will make different choices." Citing *Wisconsin v. Yoder*, which recognized that the distinctive nature of the religion of the Amish required respect and accommodation even though it was different, the dissenters write, "A way of life that is odd or even erratic but interferes with no rights or interests of others is not to be condemned because it is different." So too here, they argue: the "fundamental interest all individuals have in controlling the nature of their intimate associations with others" cannot be abridged for a minority just because a majority doesn't like them.

Bowers was argued under the Due Process Clause, and it is primarily a case about liberty. Liberty, however, in our constitutional tradition, is closely linked to equality, because fundamental liberties (of speech, religion, etc.) are not secured to individuals unless they are secured on a basis of equality. In the law of religion, for example, it has long been recognized that defending religious liberty requires more than not persecuting people: it also requires making sure that the conditions of liberty are the same for all. Similarly, the issue in *Bowers* involved both liberty and equal liberty. As Justice Stevens pointed out in his dissenting opinion, the sodomy law can be defended only in one of two ways: either homosexuals have unequal liberty interests, or there is a reason why the state is permitted to enforce a generally applicable law unevenly. The first defense is unacceptable because it violates the basic tenet of equality; the second because the state offers no argument "more substantial than a habitual dislike for, or ignorance about, the disfavored group." Similarly, Justice Blackmun makes the Millian point that "the mere knowledge that other individuals do not adhere to one's value system cannot be a legally cognizable interest" in the absence of "real interference with the rights of others."

Because the dissenters raise the issue of equality, one might ask whether the case should have been argued under the Equal Protection Clause, rather than the Due Process Clause. Justice Blackmun expresses sympathy for such an approach and cites the case overturning the antimiscegenation laws as pertinently similar. Some scholars have felt that an equal protection argument is intellectually more compelling—in part because the Equal Protection Clause is progressive, not backward looking and traditionalist, as has sometimes been said of the Due Process Clause. But the Due Process Clause should not be seen as backward looking, particularly if rights are understood at a reasonable level of generality. Nor is equality the only pertinent issue here: in light of the history of equal-time repression, the liberty interest itself needs to be vindicated strongly for all.[30]

Bowers is a low point in recent Supreme Court jurisprudence. Its result and the harshness of the majority and concurring opinions not only left vital liberty interests unaddressed but also gave comfort to the idea that gays are outlaws. In its restriction of fundamental individual rights in the name of majority prejudice, the case resembles such ugly cases from the past as *Plessy v. Fergusson*,[31] which upheld the constitutionality of racial segregation, and *Bradwell v. Illinois*,[32] which upheld an Illinois law forbidding women to practice law. A famous concurring opinion in the case cited widespread moral judgments about the proper role of women in society. Perhaps even more uncannily similar is *Minersville v. Gobitis*,[33] which upheld a compulsory flag-salute law against a challenge from Jehovah's Witnesses, who refuse the salute on religious grounds. The suggestion that Witnesses were outlaws and subversives (if they obeyed their conscience) let loose an ugly torrent of violence against them across the nation.[34] That violence, together with the general condemnation of the opinion, led to a reconsideration only three years later.[35] Gays and lesbians had to wait a lot longer.

5. *LAWRENCE V. TEXAS:* TOWARD A REGIME OF EQUAL LIBERTY

The political struggle now moved to the states. By 1996, more than half of the states that had sodomy laws at the time of *Bowers* had repealed them. The number of states with such laws declined to sixteen by the time they were all invalidated, in 2003. These repeals were part of a general change in social attitudes. Americans were becoming more aware of gays and lesbians as full human beings—in families, in the workplace, in churches, in the media, in every part of the fabric of American society. The closet had enabled the politics of disgust, making it possible to portray gays and lesbians as unlike ordinary citizens. Coming out, together with the daily operations of imagination, concern, and friendship, had a large effect on people's views.

On September 17, 1998, John Geddes Lawrence, a medical technologist, age fifty-five, was having consensual anal sex with Tyron Garner in Lawrence's Houston apartment. Unbeknownst to him, a neighbor, Robert Royce Eubanks, who had earlier been accused of harassing Lawrence and Garner, and who had a romantic relationship with Garner, phoned in a complaint of a "weapons disturbance" in Lawrence's home, saying that a man with a gun was "going crazy." (Eubanks later admitted that he had been lying and served fifteen days in jail for filing a false police report.) When the police arrived, they entered the unlocked apartment with weapons drawn and arrested the two men. They were held overnight in jail and charged with violating Texas's sodomy law. Pleading no contest, they were convicted by a justice of the peace, but they then exercised their right to a new trial and asked the court to dismiss the charges against them. They cited both equal protection grounds (given that Texas's law prohibits sodomy only between same-sex partners) and Due Process liberty grounds. In December 2002, the Supreme Court agreed to hear the case. On June 26, 2003, by a 6–3 vote, the Court found in favor of Lawrence and Garner, overruling *Bowers v. Hardwick* and invalidating all the extant state sodomy laws.

For Justice O'Connor, who wrote a concurring opinion, the salient issue was equality. Justice O'Connor, who had voted with the majority in *Bowers*, did not express a view on the question of whether a neutral sodomy law would be unconstitutional on due process grounds; she argued that this issue need not be decided, since the Texas law was plainly unconstitutional on Equal Protection grounds. Citing *Cleburne* as a precedent, she argued that the state may not single out a class of citizens for special disadvantages simply because many people disapprove of or dislike them. "Moral disapproval of a group cannot be a legitimate governmental interest under the Equal Protection clause."

Justice O'Connor's opinion shows us both the promise and the limitation of an equal protection approach: it suffices to invalidate the law in question, and perhaps it would also suffice to invalidate neutral laws if it were shown that they were unequally enforced. But it does not address the more fundamental issue of intrusiveness and decisional liberty.

The majority, however, decided that the time had come to articulate boldly the nature of the liberty interest in intimate association. *Bowers*, they held, "was not correct when it was decided, and it is not correct today." The *Bowers* majority had framed the liberty interest wrongly and narrowly. Correctly seen, *Lawrence*, like *Bowers*, involves the government's role in intimate personal relationships. "Liberty protects the person from unwarranted government intrusions into a dwelling or other private places....Liberty presumes an autonomy of self that includes freedom of thought, belief, expression, and certain intimate conduct." Justice Kennedy's opinion for the Court argues that private and consensual conduct is within the liberty of all persons to choose without being branded as criminals.

This is a correct and powerful interpretation of the liberty interests protected by the Due Process Clause. Justice Kennedy is also on strong ground when he observes that due process liberties have an equality aspect, and also that the equality interest cannot be well served by a narrow approach through the idea of equal protection alone.[36] Only a robust protection of liberty for all will eliminate the stigma inflicted by sodomy laws.

Equality by itself, without appeal to protected areas of liberty, is insufficient, because government can infringe on vital liberties with an even hand. Laws that say, for example, that no couple, married or unmarried, can have more than one child; laws that prohibit marriage between people of different religions; laws that prohibit masturbation: such laws probably don't offend against the Equal Protection Clause, but they are offensive. The core idea of a protected area of liberty is independent of and not fully explained by the idea of equal treatment: we need an account of which liberties are protected, before we say that liberties are protected equally for all.

Lawrence articulates well the relevant notions of liberty and equal liberty. Nonetheless, the resonant opinion suffers from the salient defect of some of its predecessors: it relies unduly on the murky notion of privacy. At least *Lawrence* recognizes that privacy has two aspects, the decisional and the spatial. After initial references to "a dwelling or other private places" and "the home," Justice Kennedy immediately writes that the case "involves liberty of the person both in its spatial and more transcendent dimensions," and he grants that "there are other spheres of our lives and existence, outside the home, where the State should not be a dominant presence." Even with this distinction stated, however, the opinion goes on to rely on the spatial notion of privacy at key moments, thus suggesting a constitutional approach that is both overprotective and underprotective. The state does, of course, have a role in the home—when harm is in the offing. Nor is it clear why the fact that the sex act performed by Lawrence and Garner was in "the home" should be relevant. Surely, the relevant issue is one of the interests of other parties: no nonconsenting party's rights are being violated, and, because the conduct took place in seclusion, no nonconsenting party is being subjected to direct offense.

That is all that needed to be said. "The home" is a red herring. Bill Baird (of *Eisenstadt v. Baird*) gave contraceptives to undergraduates at a public meeting. What was important was that he violated nobody's rights and inflicted no damage on unwilling bystanders. More generally, countless contraceptive acts protected by the Fourteenth Amendment take place outside the home, in public places— every time, for example, a woman takes her pill with lunch or dinner in a restaurant, or goes to a public restroom to insert a diaphragm. For that matter, even in *Griswold*, where the marital home is mentioned as salient, the plaintiffs were practitioners who had prescribed contraceptives and offered contraceptive advice in their medical offices. The relevant issues are consent and offense, not location.

As for actual sex acts, where there is always the potential for a type of harm. Suppose that Lawrence and Garner had had sex in a hotel room instead of Lawrence's home. In this case, because of the room's homelike character, most people will immediately see that it should be similarly protected. The relevant issues, again, are consent and seclusion (removing the possibility of harm). Sex in a crowded hotel ballroom would not be protected. But what if they had had sex in a private club, either in a secluded room in that club, or in a room where nobody who did not want to watch was present? What if they had had sex in a secluded area in the woods? These questions will occupy us in chapter 6.

On these important questions, *Lawrence* offers no guidance. We don't even know whether the spatial component is meant to be a necessary element of the protected liberty interest or just one option; that's how unclear the opinion is. The references to liberty in general suggest that protection extends beyond "the home," but how far beyond, and on what principle, is left utterly unclear. And yet there was a principle readily available: Mill's idea of self-regarding conduct, which could have clearly demarcated protected intimate association from both harmful and offensive conduct.

Lawrence's great achievement, then, was not conceptual clarity or sharp practical guidance, but a cast of mind, a judicial approach to liberty interests. In essence, it consists in a rejection of the politics of disgust so amply evident in *Bowers*, together with the Devlinesque conception of society as dominated by tradition and solidarity, in favor of a politics of humanity that is the heir of John Stuart Mill both in its zealous protection of individual liberty and in its reliance on the ability to imagine a variety of human purposes. Instead of being treated as a class of outlaws condemned by the wisdom of the ages, gays and lesbians took their place, in the judicial mind, as equal citizens and "adult persons," with interests like those of other people "in deciding how to conduct their private lives in matters relating to sex." That's an achievement of the moral imagination. Because law is inseparably bound up with the moral imagination, it is also an achievement in law.

FROM DISGUST TO HUMANITY

NOTES

1. From the interview with Hardwick in Peter Irons, *The Courage of Their Convictions* (New York: Free Press, 1988), 396.

2. Mill thought of all animals as subjects of justice: thus any activity that harms existing animals was potentially regulable. His principles can easily be extended to future humans and animals. It is less clear whether a Millian principle can support the protection of endangered species, or environmental degradation that does not harm humans or animals. See my discussion in Nussbaum, *Frontiers of Justice* (Cambridge, MA: Harvard University Press, 2006), chap. 6, where I agree with Mill that the issue of justice is pertinent only to sentient creatures, but argue that other principles— intellectual, aesthetic, scientific—could justify laws protecting species and the environment. Although Mill did not write about sex with animals, we may use his principle to justify laws against bestiality—on the grounds that the animal never consents in a way that is relevant to the best legal notions of consent in sexual assault doctrine. If we once agree that sex with animals is a type of harm, however, we will be led to ask what other conduct toward animals deserves the same stricture: another reason why a politics based upon harm is more probing, whereas a politics based on disgust short-circuits the search for reasons.

3. See the discussion of nuisance law in Nussbaum, *Hiding from Humanity: Disgust, Shame, and the Law* (Princeton: Princeton University Press, 2004), chap. 3.

4. Runners often apply this principle when the city of Chicago locks the public restrooms adjacent to the running paths for winter to save money involved in cleaning them. A common practice is to use the area just behind the locked restroom, thus indicating that one would have used the restroom had it not been stupidly locked.

5. *Barnes v. Glen Theatre*, 501 U.S. 560 (1991). Notice that, although the majority opinion rested on purely Devlinesque considerations, Justice Souter's concurrence argues that nude dancing is not purely self-regarding, because it creates an atmosphere of exploitation and criminal activity. His analysis of this case is similar to Mill's argument (tentative) that keepers of gambling houses might possibly be proper subjects of legal regulation.

6. Justice Scalia has repeatedly done this, not least in this area of law.

7. France is well known for its ban on large or conspicuous religious articles of dress in public schools; but individual cities in Belgium and the Netherlands have also been passing related laws—forbidding government employees to wear such articles, for example.

8. In order to express his attitude about this difference, Mill insisted on being buried in France.

9. Statutes against "buggery" remain in force in some former parts of the British empire; in Hong Kong, for example, both same-sex and opposite-sex "buggery" laws are still on the books, despite having been found unconstitutional in 2005.

10. However, cross-dressing and using a dildo were considered fraud: see Louis Crompton, "The Myth of Lesbian Impunity: Capital Laws from 1270 to 1791," *Journal of Homosexuality* 6 (1980), 22–26.

11. The initial proposal was a one-year maximum, but legislators demanded a harsher penalty.

12. Wilde, however, was in fact married and had two children.

13. The history of Paragraph 175 is complicated by the fact that some German states had had, and repealed, sodomy laws earlier (one reason for the national legislation); the more tolerant character of Germany is shown by the fact that the Social Democratic Party almost immediately sought repeal of Paragraph 175, and a wide range of both gay and straight artists and intellectuals (including Thomas Mann, Martin Buber, Rainer Maria Rilke, Herman Hesse, and many others) publicly joined the prorepeal movement. Wilde, by contrast, had virtually no nongay defenders (apart from a couple of prominent women), and no political party ever dreamed of defending him. Paragraph 175, though strengthened by the Nazis, was rewritten as a simple age of consent law in East Germany in 1957 and in West Germany in 1969. All legal distinctions between heterosexual and homosexual acts were abolished in the East in 1988 (including differences in age of consent), and, since Reunification in 1994, this uniformity extends to all Germany.

14. Gary David Comstock, *Violence against Lesbians and Gay Men* (New York: Columbia University Press, 1991).

15. Irons, *Courage of Their Convictions*, 395.

16. *Griswold v. Connecticut*, 381 U.S. 479 (1965).

17. *Roe v. Wade*, 410 U.S. 113 (1973).

18. *Meyer v. Nebraska*, 262 U.S. 390 (1923).

19. *Pierce v. Society of Sisters*, 210 U.S. 510 (1925).

20. *Olmstead v. U.S.*, 277 U.S. 438 (1928). The case concerned wiretapping of private phone conversations.

21. *Eisenstadt v. Baird*, 405 U.S. 438 (1972).

22. Here I draw on Nussbaum, "Sex Equality, Liberty, and Privacy: A Comparative Approach to the Feminist Critique," in *India's Living Constitution: Ideas, Practices, Controversies*, volume from conference on the fiftieth anniversary of the Indian Constitution, ed. E. Sridharan, Z. Hasan, and R. Sudarshan (New Delhi: Permanent Black, 2002), 242–83. A shortened version was published under the title "What's Privacy Got to Do with It? A Comparative Approach to the Feminist Critique," in *Women and the United States Constitution: History, Interpretation, Practice*, ed. Sibyl A. Schwarzenbach and Patricia Smith (New York: Columbia University Press, 2003), 153–75. See also the excellent discussion of the limits of the concept in relation to sexual liberty in Kendall Thomas, "Beyond the Privacy Principle," *Columbia Law Review* 92 (1992), 1431–1516.

23. 394 U.S. 557 (1969).

24. Compounding the confusion is the fact that two years later, in *U.S. v. Reidel*, 402 U.S. 351 (1971), the Court made it clear that *Stanley* did not call into question prevailing laws against the distribution of obscenity: so you could use it in the privacy of your home, but virtually every means of acquiring the material can be punished.

25. *Moore v. East Cleveland*, 431 U.S. 494, 503 (1977).

26. *Palko v. Connecticut*, 302 U.S. 319, 325, 236 (1937).

27. *Powell v. Alabama*, 287 U.S. 45, 67 (1932).

28. All the narrative detail in this section is from the Irons interview.

29. See Linda Greenhouse, "Washington Talk: When Second Thoughts in Case Come Too Late," *New York Times*, November 5, 1990; Powell, talking to students at NYU, said, "I think I probably made a mistake."

30. See Kenji Yoshino, "Tribe," forthcoming, *Tulsa Law Review* 42 (2007), 961–73; in *"Lawrence v. Texas*: The Fundamental Right that Dare Not Speak Its Name," *Harvard Law Review* 117 (2004), 1893–1955, Tribe argues that the Due Process Clause itself has an equality aspect, in that it is used to invalidate the unequal protection of fundamental rights.

31. 163 U.S. 537 (1896).

32. 83 U.S. 130 (1873).

33. 310 U. S 586 (1940).

34. See Nussbaum, *Liberty of Conscience: In Defense of America's Tradition of Religious Equality* (New York: Basic Books, 2007), chap. 5.

35. *West Virginia Board of Education v. Barnette*, 319 U.S. 624 (1943).

36. See Tribe, *"Lawrence v. Texas."*

CHAPTER FOUR

Discrimination and Antidiscrimination:
Romer and Animus

Militant gays want government to give their lifestyle special class status—but we think it's important to know just what kind of lifestyle they want your tax dollars to endorse. You may already know that the sexual practices of gays differ drastically from those of most of Colorado's population. But how much these practices differ—and the dangerous perversions they involve—may shock you!

Gays have been unwilling (or unable) to curb their voracious, unsafe sex practices in the face of AIDS.... Overall, surveys show that 90% of gay men engage in anal intercourse—the most high-risk sexual behavior in society today.... About 80% of gay men surveyed have engaged in oral sex upon the anus of partners. Well over a third of gays in 1977 admitted to "fisting." ... Is this the kind of lifestyle we want to reward with special protection, and protected ethnic status? Gay activists want you to think they're "just like you"—but these statistics point out how false that is.

PAMPHLET CIRCULATED BY *COLORADO FOR FAMILY VALUES* DURING
THE CAMPAIGN FOR COLORADO'S AMENDMENT 2

We find nothing special in the protections Amendment 2 withholds. These are protections taken for granted by most people either because they already have them or do not need them; these are protections against exclusion from an almost limitless number of transactions and endeavors that constitute ordinary civic life in a free society.

MAJORITY OPINION, ROMER V. EVANS, 1996

I. FAMILY VALUES AND ANTIDISCRIMINATION LAWS

Will Perkins is a Chrysler dealer in Colorado Springs, Colorado. Early in the 1990s, he was recruited to the board of Colorado for Family Values (CFV), a conservative organization founded by Tony Marco, a fundraiser for conservative religious groups, and Kevin Tebedo, son of a lobbyist for similar causes. (Tebedo was fired by CFV in 1995, during a scandal over his defense of a pastor who purported to cure homosexuality but who was then accused of child molestation.) The current (2009) CFV website describes it as "a non-profit advocacy group dedicated to preserving, protecting, and defending traditional family values."[1]

CFV decided that its first large initiative would be a statewide referendum banning local gay-rights laws. Perkins was recruited to chair this campaign and to bankroll much of the early effort. Perkins then enlisted former U.S. Senator Bill Armstrong and popular University of Colorado football coach, Bill McCartney. The group hired Paul Cameron to advise them on strategy.

Like most states, Colorado houses a great deal of social and political diversity. Larger cities such as Denver and Boulder, and wealthy enclaves such as Aspen, tend to have a liberal character. All three of these cities (and the County of Denver, in a separate ordinance) had passed broad antidiscrimination laws that included sexual orientation (along with race, sex, age, and many other categories) as a prohibited ground of discrimination, in "housing, employment, education, public accommodations, health and welfare services, and other transactions and activities."[2] Rural areas of the state are more conservative, and Colorado Springs is a headquarters for many Christian conservative groups, which it actively recruits through favorable policies.

Christian conservatives, in the early 1990s, had grounds for concern. The three city ordinances were problematic, but even more ominous were developments at the state level. The state legislature repealed Colorado's sodomy law in 1972, and antidiscrimination efforts had recently picked up steam. In 1990, popular Governor Roy Romer signed an executive order protecting state government workers from discrimination based on sexual orientation.[3] In 1991, a state law targeting hate crimes against gays and lesbians was proposed, and even Colorado Springs saw the introduction of an antidiscrimination law. Although both measures failed, they gave an unsettling impression of social change.[4]

For Perkins and Marco, rolling back the forward march of what they repeatedly called "militant gay aggression" was an issue of the utmost urgency. According to Perkins, homosexuals have "a radically deviant obsession with sex" and are responsible for an overwhelming proportion of child molestation. Indeed, he charged in a CFV pamphlet that "sexual molestation of children is a large part of many homosexuals' lifestyle."[5]

On March 20, 1992, Perkins arrived at the Colorado State House in an armored car, from which he produced petitions containing eighty-five thousand signatures. He declared, "We consider these to be among the most important pieces of paper in the entire United States."[6] The signatures Perkins had gathered were more than sufficient to put Amendment 2 on the ballot.

Legitimate concerns can be raised about antidiscrimination laws in general and those involving sexual orientation in particular. People with strong religious beliefs are plausibly concerned that antidiscrimination laws will force religious organizations to hire people of whom some religions disapprove. This issue is not peculiar to sexual orientation. It may arise, for example, when such laws seem to force a religious organization to hire people who don't belong to that religion. In 1987, the Supreme Court ruled that the Church of Jesus Christ of Latter-Day Saints was not prevented by federal nondiscrimination laws from firing a janitor from his job in the Salt Lake City temple because he was not a Mormon.[7] Even though being a janitor was not a religious function, the Court reasoned that attempting to make a distinction between religious and nonreligious functions would involve the Court in intrusive policing of religious institutions. The Court made clear that religious institutions enjoy considerable latitude to favor coreligionists, despite federal antidiscrimination legislation.

It remains debatable to what extent religious objections should exempt religious organizations from antidiscrimination laws when the issue is not religion but race or gender or sexual orientation or marital status. It is also controversial to what extent individuals (as opposed to religious organizations) may claim religiously based exemptions from antidiscrimination laws. (Cases involving landlords unwilling to rent to unmarried heterosexual couples on religious grounds have caused controversy in several states.) Both Denver and Aspen had shown their concern for this issue by crafting their ordinances to give exemptions for religious objections. If the purpose of Amendment 2 were to guarantee that religious opinions about sexual orientation were sufficiently respected, it could have been written so as to require all antidiscrimination laws and orders to have similar escape clauses.

Similarly, a worry might be raised about personal associational freedom. Suppose landlords in small owner-occupied rental buildings were required to rent to tenants of whose way of life they disapprove, whether on religious or on moral grounds. If one were worried about that issue, one could propose a law exempting small buildings (or even small family-operated businesses) from the scope of antidiscrimination laws.

More generally, an organization devoted to family values might legitimately worry about the future of families, understood along conservative Christian lines, in an era of rapid social change. It might seek to use the law to further the interests of such families. A likely strategy would be to seek state subsidy for drug and alcohol treatment and for marriage counseling, because we know that marriages often come apart because of substance abuse or lack of pertinent counseling. One might also propose legislation strengthening penalties for an ex-spouse's avoidance of child support payments, something that is badly needed to protect vulnerable children. One might consider measures to enhance family and medical leave time from work, thus easing burdens of child and elder care. In short, as District Judge Jeffrey Bayless memorably said, "Seemingly, if one wished to promote family values, action would be taken that is pro-family rather than anti some other group."

Amendment 2, the ballot measure proposed by CFV, chose none of these approaches. Instead, it proposed a highly general disqualification of gays and lesbians from the benefits of antidiscrimination protections:

> No Protected Status Based on Homosexual, Lesbian, or Bisexual Orientation. Neither the State of Colorado, through any of its branches or departments, nor any of its agencies, political subdivisions, municipalities or school districts, shall enact, adopt or enforce any statute, regulation, ordinance or policy whereby homosexual, lesbian or bisexual orientation, conduct, practices or relationships shall constitute or otherwise be the basis of or

entitle any person or class of persons to have or claim any minority status, quota preferences, protected status or claim of discrimination. This Section of the Constitution shall be in all respects self-executing.

What would Amendment 2 have accomplished if implemented? As the Colorado Supreme Court analyzed the referendum:

> The immediate objective of Amendment 2 is, at a minimum, to repeal existing statutes, regulations, ordinances, and policies of state and local entities that barred discrimination based on sexual orientation. [a list of these is now given, including the ordinances in Denver, Boulder, and Aspen, and also including Romer's Executive Order and a similar provision of the Colorado Insurance Code]; and various provisions prohibiting discrimination based on sexual orientation at state colleges.
>
> [examples again given]
>
> The "ultimate effect" of Amendment 2 is to prohibit any governmental entity from adopting similar, or more protective statutes, regulations, ordinances, or policies in the future unless the state constitution is first amended to permit such measures.

Nor are these changes limited to what is traditionally called the "public sphere": nondiscrimination laws are binding on private as well as public employment and in places that qualify as places of "public accommodation." (The Boulder ordinance, for example, defined such places as "any place of business engaged in any sales to the general public and any place that offers services, facilities, privileges, or advantages to the general public or that receives financial support through solicitation of the general public or through governmental subsidy of any kind.") Landlords are also affected, if they offer enough units to count as a public accommodation, a definition that varies from place to place. In addition, specific legal protections for gays and lesbians in all transactions in housing, real estate, health and welfare services, and private employment would be abolished.

So, the amendment would reach widely, denying many ordinary privileges of life in a democratic society to gays and lesbians, and preventing gays and lesbians from bringing legal action against any form of discrimination, however invidious. That, indeed, was just the point. The changes envisaged in Amendment 2 are sweeping. Gays and lesbians are singled out from all others and put in a special class of their own: only they may not seek or enjoy specific legal protection from discrimination.

But surely Amendment 2 denies them "special rights," not equal rights. Such was always the rhetoric of its proponents. But let's think a minute. Why do communities pass laws protecting a group from discrimination? They don't do so just to be nice, but because there is a perceived problem: enough of the general public feels that discrimination against members of the group warrants changes in the law.

Let's just imagine, now, a 1960 Mississippi version of Amendment 2, let's call it Amendment M, a referendum that would debar African-Americans (and only them) from protected status under state and local nondiscrimination laws. Let's suppose that its proponents keep saying, "Equal rights, not special rights": we don't hate African-Americans, we just want to deny them *special* rights.

We see right away that this referendum would not be a neutral measure designed to restore all citizens to a plane of equality. It would be a racist measure, designed to prevent African-Americans from availing themselves of legal protections that they had won because citizens saw a problem of discrimination and decided to remedy it. By mentioning African-Americans as a group not entitled to seek antidiscrimination protection, the law singles them out from all others. It doesn't simply have an impact that affects them more than others (as would an amendment prohibiting laws against discrimination on the basis of race). It names them as the one group that cannot turn to the law for protection against discrimination. All other groups—Italian-Americans, Roman Catholics, cyclists, animal-lovers, smokers, people over sixty, and any other groups you like to imagine—all those could mobilize to seek protection from discrimination. Only African-Americans could not do so. Wouldn't we think that African-Americans were being stigmatized in a unique manner and denied the status, under the law, that other citizens enjoy? Amendment 2 is the equivalent of Amendment M. CFV was not proposing a narrow measure targeted at protecting religious citizens, or traditional families; it was proposing a wide and open-ended set of disabilities for gays and lesbians, named as a targeted group (even those who never have sex at all, since the amendment carefully included both status and conduct).

Amendment 2 expresses a Devlinesque conception of society: what the average person views with strong disapproval, he is entitled to discourage by law. Amendment 2 asks voters to express strong emotion about sexual orientation, and then makes that indignation the basis for widespread legal disadvantages. As for the Millian idea that the fully equal rights of individuals should not be abridged just because lots of people don't like what they imagine these people are doing, that idea is left on the outside looking in. It would be the business of the *Romer v. Evans* litigation to reinstate it.

The contest began. Perkins, Marco, and their allies had raised quite a lot of money (with Perkins a primary contributor), and leafleting began all across the state. The campaign was clever. On the whole, it did not foreground the appeal to naked disgust or dislike. The leading theme was always that of "equal rights, not special rights." That gave ordinary citizens a reason to support the referendum without thinking that in so doing they were expressing dislike of gays and lesbians. Many citizens surely supported the referendum for these other reasons—prominently including members of other protected minorities who feared that antidiscrimination laws mentioning sexual orientation would sap the protections their groups already enjoyed (for example, by encouraging state expenditure on other nondiscrimination efforts that might take money and support from their own).

Many citizens of good will also voted for the referendum because they were simply confused by the length and complexity of the measure: exit polls showed that a significant number didn't understand on which side they were voting.

It cannot be doubted, however, that the appeal to disgust was a major part of what carried the day. CFV literature foregrounded "equal rights not special rights." It even repeated slogans such as "Hate is not a family value."[8] But material about the degenerate lives and horrible sex practices of gays and lesbians was always present, as with the passage I quoted from one typical leaflet, where it was conveniently positioned right next to the column titled "Hate is not a family value." I personally heard the testimony of Will Perkins in the bench trial of Amendment 2 on October 15, 1993. I heard him admit (somewhat reluctantly) to circulating yet other pamphlets that mentioned the classic Cameron claim that gays eat feces and drink raw blood. The proponents hired Cameron to help direct their strategy, well aware of his views.

Was the appeal to disgust just an extra add-on, or was it a central part of the strategy? Perkins and Marco frequently used disgust language, and related terms such as "depraved" and "deviant." They also gave Cameron a central place in their campaign—as the state's attorney general later gave him a central place in its defense of the amendment. Their speeches talked about disease, about child molestation, about "militant gay aggression." Above all, they sought to extinguish any sense of empathy or commonality with gays and lesbians by continually insisting that their practices "differ drastically" from those of average Coloradans. Promoting disgust and undermining a "politics of humanity" went hand in hand. So if the material about sex practices was not always front and center, it was important. The strategy was to give voters lots of reasons to feel disgust—but then to give them, as well, more socially acceptable reasons for voting "yes," which they could use to justify their vote to both self and others.

On November 3, 1992, Amendment 2 passed by a vote of 813,966 to 710,151 (53.4 percent to 46.6 percent). Immediately, a group of plaintiffs—including individuals (Martina Navratilova was one), and numerous governmental entities (the Boulder Valley School District, the City and County of Denver, the City of Boulder, the City of Aspen, and the City Council of Aspen) began contesting the law, hoping to prevent its implementation.

2. ACT I: COLORADO—FUNDAMENTAL RIGHTS AND THE POLITICAL PROCESS

The litigation surrounding Amendment 2 was complicated, involving three distinct legal theories. Following these will give us further insight into what support for the amendment was really about and why its rejection by the Supreme Court was right.

Act I of the drama was the plaintiffs' motion, before District Court Judge H. Jeffrey Bayless, for a preliminary injunction against the implementation of the law. Throughout the initial phases, the plaintiffs were trying to find a way of ensuring that the state would have to show not simply a rational basis for the law, but a compelling state interest. Most laws are upheld on rational basis review, so, despite the fact that the plaintiffs consistently argued that the law lacked even a rational basis, a key part of their strategy was to devise some theory that would move Amendment 2 into the category of laws for which heightened scrutiny was required.

There are two ways in which such an argument may be made under the Equal Protection Clause of the Fourteenth Amendment. First, one can argue that classification of people on the basis of their sexual orientation is a suspect classification, an idea explored in chapter 2. That strategy seemed unlikely to succeed, because it had not succeeded in other cases. Second, one can argue, as we saw in chapter 3, that the challenged law infringes one of the unenumerated "fundamental rights" that have been recognized as inherent in the Equal Protection Clause, such as the right to vote and the right to travel.

During act 1, the plaintiffs elaborated a clever version of the latter strategy, which was endorsed by the Colorado Supreme Court.[9] They argued that Amendment 2 deprives gays and lesbians of the right to "participate equally in the political process," by "fencing" them "out" from the opportunity, which all other citizens enjoy, to pass local and state laws protecting their interests. They rested this argument on a group of cases involving reapportionment, minority party rights, and various other attempts to "limit the ability of certain groups to have desired legislation implemented through the normal political processes." The Colorado Supreme Court argued that, although the precedents all involved race, the core of the argument did not rest on the notion of racially suspect classification, but rather, on the principle that the Equal Protection Clause "guarantees the fundamental right to participate equally in the political process and that any attempt to infringe on an independently identifiable group's ability to exercise that right is subject to strict judicial scrutiny."

This was an interesting legal theory, but it had its problems. First of all, the ballot-access and right to vote cases were being stretched, in order to find a general right to participate as equals in the political process.[10] More puzzling was the theory's use of the notion of "an independently identifiable group." Obviously this

could not mean only those groups who already enjoyed suspect classification status, or gays and lesbians would be excluded. On the
other hand, one would have to find some way of demarcating the
notion of "independently identifiable," or the theory would sweep
too broadly. (Many laws discriminate against felons, for example,
and the Colorado Supreme Court certainly did not intend to call
those laws into question.) The court tried to demarcate the notion,
suggesting that it includes only groups who traditionally have been
protected under antidiscrimination laws or would benefit from such
protections. It's not clear, however, that this makes "independently
identifiable" into a workable notion.

More problematic was the relationship of this legal theory to
Bowers v. Hardwick. According to *Bowers*, gays and lesbians can
rightly be stigmatized as criminals. But of course many provisions,
thought to be constitutional, disadvantage criminals in the political
process. Take, for example, the laws on the books in many states
that remove the vote from convicted felons. If gays are or can legally
be made criminals, can't they be treated unequally in the political
process? We could try to distinguish between act and orientation,
saying that it's wrong to treat people of homosexual orientation
unequally, even though there is a very strong likelihood that they
routinely commit criminal acts (or acts that may be criminalized).
This has always been a murky distinction, however.

Evans 1 was a ringing victory for the plaintiffs, but one whose
legal credentials seemed flimsy.

3. ACT 2: THE BENCH TRIAL—ANIMUS ON PARADE

By upholding the preliminary injunction against the law, the Colorado Supreme Court had simply returned it to the District Court for
a trial on the merits. Act 2 of the drama, then, returns us to the

Denver courtroom of District Judge H. Jeffrey Bayless. It was now clear (under the traditional standards for heightened scrutiny) that the state would have to demonstrate that Amendment 2 served a "compelling state interest," and that it was the narrowest and least burdensome way of protecting that interest.

The plaintiffs, however, also wanted Judge Bayless to rule that sexual orientation is a suspect classification. On that issue, the plaintiffs failed. They called a range of expert witnesses to demonstrate that gays and lesbians, as a class, have the three characteristics that have traditionally served as criteria of a suspect classification: a history of discrimination, political powerlessness, and the immutability of the class's defining characteristic. Judge Bayless found the plaintiffs' argument persuasive on the first issue, and both strong and interesting on the third, although he made no final determination. The argument that gays and lesbians are politically powerless, however, failed to convince him: the very laws that Amendment 2 nullified were proof, he said, of gays' and lesbians' substantial political power. In the end, Judge Bayless refused to conclude that sexual orientation was a suspect classification.

Most of the action in the trial therefore focused on the state's attempt to demonstrate that Amendment 2 served a compelling state interest. The strategy of Colorado Attorney General Gale Norton was blunt and aggressive: line up as many compelling interests as possible, then bring in academic experts to testify in support of each.

Six compelling interests were originally alleged: (1) deterring factionalism (by which the state meant that political debate over this "deeply divisive" issue would be removed from local governments); (2) preserving the integrity of the state's political functions—allegedly at risk from "militant gay aggression"; (3) preserving the state's ability to remedy discrimination against traditional suspect classes; (4) preventing the government from interfering with personal, familial, and religious privacy; (5) preventing government from subsidizing the political objectives of a special interest group; and (6) promoting the physical and psychological well-being of children. The state argued that each of these, taken singly, was compelling, and that, even if none was compelling taken singly, they might be found compelling in the aggregate. In addition, at a relatively late point in the trial, a seventh allegedly compelling interest, in "public morality," was added. The state claimed that it pervaded all the other six.

Judge Bayless ultimately found that interest 1 was not compelling: indeed, he wrote that "[t]he *opposite* of defendants' first claimed compelling interest is most probably compelling," in the sense that vigorous political debate at the local level, not the removal of that debate, is a compelling interest.[11] He also found that interest 2 was not compelling: "The evidence presented does not satisfy this court that there is militant gay aggression in this state which endangers the state's political functions." The third alleged compelling interest amounted to the claim that the state doesn't have enough resources to protect an extra group from discrimination, without taking money away from efforts to aid already protected groups. Judge Bayless found that the testimony of Denver's mayor and of the officer in charge of enforcing Denver's antidiscrimination ordinance established that "[t]he inclusion of sexual orientation in the Denver ordinance has not necessitated an increase of enforcement staff nor has it resulted in an increase in costs."

The fourth compelling interest was a different story. Clearly, the protection of religious freedom is a compelling state interest. Amendment 2, however, Judge Bayless held, is not narrowly tailored so as to achieve that interest in the "least restrictive manner possible": what the state could do was to require antidiscrimination provisions to contain a religious exemption, as Denver's and Aspen's already did.

The fifth alleged interest concerned the way in which, according to the state, people would be forced to accept the "gay ideology" by complying with nondiscrimination laws. "For example," wrote the state in its trial brief, "if a landlord is forced to rent an apartment to a homosexual couple, the landlord is being forced to accept, at least implicitly, a particular ideology." Bayless concluded that this alleged compelling interest "was not supported by any credible evidence or any cogent argument."

The sixth alleged compelling interest was the promotion of the physical and psychological well-being of children. Testimony had been offered by expert witnesses for the state suggesting that homosexuals are often child molesters. To this, Bayless responded that the extensive testimony of a reputable psychologist called by the plaintiffs showed convincingly that pedophiles are predominantly heterosexual; thus the defendants had not established this claimed compelling interest. Finally, Bayless did not address the public morality issue directly; he simply concluded at this point that the state had not met the requirements that strict scrutiny imposes.

Those were the interests and the outcome. In between was expert testimony, designed to support the claims of compelling state interest. It was here that the bench trial of Amendment 2 became circuslike. The state, advised by Paul Cameron (to whom, it later emerged, Norton paid more than $10,000 of state money for his help in the case) rounded up a remarkable group of witnesses to support its claims.[12] On the issues of child molestation and family values, the extreme views of Cameron shaped the witness list, and several state experts shared with Cameron the characteristic of having been expelled from, or denounced by, a respected professional organization for views that flew in the face of the evidence, or (as with Cameron) for manufacturing evidence.[13] Cameron himself was on the witness list. (He was never put on the stand, but his expert witness statement became part of the trial record.) The state seemed eager to call as a witness any reasonably well-known scholar who would say something bad about gays and lesbians.

Expert testimony is not truth seeking. Each side will properly call experts who support its views. Nonetheless, there was still something ugly about the experts called by the state, many of whom were known to be discredited. The same antigay sentiment that had gained passage of Amendment 2 shaped the state's defense of the law.

Oddest and perhaps most revealing was the testimony about "public morality," most of which had no relevance to the case. The state, presumably aware that its expert social scientists were not distinguished, learned that a few genuinely eminent intellectuals wanted to testify about moral philosophy and its history, hoping to establish that gays had been found depraved and unacceptable by all the world's great thinkers.

The primary witnesses who testified in this arm of the trial were: philosopher John Finnis of Oxford University (now also at the University of Notre Dame); political theorist Robert George of Princeton University; philosopher David Novak of the University of Toronto (then at the University of Virginia); and political theorist Harvey Mansfield of Harvard University. Novak offered a scholarly and closely reasoned account of the tradition of Jewish thought that, while controversial, was in the scholarly mainstream.[14] Nor did Novak ever claim that his historical material had any bearing on what modern democracies should do. The other three witnesses, however, were zealous in their defense of Amendment 2 and in their contention that the history of thought supported the law. They offered an odd concoction of claims. Robert George, an advocate of a conservative variety of Catholic natural law teaching, revealed in his testimony that he believed same-sex acts to be bad for just the reasons and in the way that contraception and masturbation are bad; he urged that landlords be permitted to refuse to rent to tenants who would practice either—a position so extreme that it surely had no relevance to establishing "public morality" in Colorado. Harvard's Mansfield testified that homosexuality is a pathological and miserable lifestyle that always leads to deep unhappiness.[15] (It's not terribly clear how this supported an amendment that was likely to make gays in Colorado more unhappy than they were before.) He supported all sorts of comparative claims about the happiness of gays and lesbians (vis-à-vis African-Americans and women) by citing the great books of the Western tradition of political philosophy— naming Rousseau, Tocqueville, Plato, and Aristotle, despite the fact that such comparisons were never discussed by those thinkers.

4. ACT 3: THE SUPREME COURT—ANIMUS AND RATIONAL BASIS

The state appealed to the Colorado Supreme Court, which found Amendment 2 unconstitutional on the same ground it had mapped out in its first opinion.[16] Colorado appealed to the U.S. Supreme Court, which agreed to hear the case.

At this point, the issue of strategy became all-important for the plaintiffs. The fundamental rights strategy was risky, because of Bowers. To avoid a head-on challenge to Bowers, the plaintiffs argued that Amendment 2 had no rational basis, invoking Cleburne and Department of Agriculture v. Moreno, [17] in which the Court had found laws to lack a rational basis if they were motivated by dislike or fear of an unpopular group. In Moreno, which concerned a requirement of the federal food stamp program that aid could go only to households that contained no member who was "unrelated" to other members, the Court wrote, "[I]f the constitutional conception of 'equal protection of the laws' means anything, it must at the very least mean that a bare...desire to harm a politically unpopular group cannot constitute a legitimate governmental interest."[18]

On May 20, 1996, the Supreme Court held Amendment 2 unconstitutional by a vote of six to three. Justice Kennedy, writing for the majority, sees the case as going directly to the heart of the Equal Protection Clause and the rule of law: that our Constitution "'neither knows nor tolerates classes among citizens'" He opened his opinion with this quote from Justice Harlan's dissenting opinion in *Plessy v. Ferguson* (1896), the notorious case in which the Supreme Court upheld the constitutionality of segregation in public accommodations—thus connecting *Romer* with our nation's long struggle against hierarchical arrangements that systematically subordinate groups.

The balance of the unusually brief opinion is devoted to an analysis of the disqualifications imposed by Amendment 2, in order to establish that they do create such a hierarchy. Kennedy rejects as implausible the state's argument that the amendment did no more than deny homosexual "special rights" (a reading accepted by Justice Scalia in his dissenting opinion). "Sweeping and comprehensive is the change in legal status effected by this law.... Homosexuals, by state decree, are put in a solitary class with respect to transactions and relations in both the private and governmental spheres." Kennedy then documents in detail the areas in which systematic inequality would result from Amendment 2.

Justice Kennedy then recognizes that most laws classify, with the result that some people are disadvantaged. For this reason, except when a law concerns a fundamental right or a suspect class, the classification is typically upheld "so long as it bears a rational relation to some legitimate end." Amendment 2, however, fails that test: it imposes broad and sweeping disqualifications on a group in every area of life, and these disqualifications are utterly discontinuous with the reasons offered for the law. Therefore "the amendment seems inexplicable by anything but animus toward the class that it affects; it lacks a rational relationship to legitimate state interests." The amendment is both too narrow and too broad: "It identifies persons by a single trait and then denies them protection across the board. The resulting disqualification of a class of persons from the right to seek specific protection from the law is unprecedented in our jurisprudence.... It is not within our constitutional tradition to enact laws of this sort."

Justice Scalia's dissenting opinion, noting that sodomy laws were held constitutional in *Bowers*, invokes a notorious case called *Davis v. Beason* (1890) to suggest that it is permissible to impose general disqualifications on a group if practices characteristic of the group can be made criminal. In *Davis*, the Court upheld an Idaho law denying polygamists, advocates of polygamy, and members of any organization that teaches or advocates polygamy (hence all Mormons) the right to vote and hold office. Justice Scalia reasoned that if Mormons can be denied the right to vote because of their likely or characteristic practices, then the disqualifications Amendment 2 imposes on gays and lesbians must also be constitutional.

It's rather shocking to see Justice Scalia relying on *Davis*, surely one of the most criticized, indeed abhorred, decisions in the history of the Supreme Court. As Justice Kennedy points out, *Davis* is no longer good law insofar as it denies the right to vote based upon belief. All that remains of *Davis* is the idea that a convicted felon may be denied the right to vote: but that was not what was at issue in considering Amendment 2. (For one thing, as we already noted, sodomy was no longer illegal in Colorado.)

As for the possibility that religious concerns could justify Amendment 2, Justice Kennedy concluded that a far narrower remedy (religious exemptions) could handle that concern. In its sweeping breadth, Amendment 2 is plainly not directed at any legitimate purpose. The only inference one can make is that the real purpose of Amendment 2 is to make homosexuals unequal to everyone else. Kennedy insisted: "This Colorado cannot do. A State cannot so deem a class of persons a stranger to its laws."

Because Justice Kennedy's opinion is so brief, it has given rise to a lot of questions. Is the main issue that of illegitimate intent? Or is the sweeping nature of the hierarchy imposed by Amendment 2 itself an equal protection violation, no matter what the animating purpose? I side with those scholars who hold that illegitimate intent or purpose is at the heart of the analysis.[19] The sweeping nature of the disqualifications is important, but it is important heuristically, in revealing that the purpose of the amendment is not what the state claims, namely the protection of religious freedom or the restoration of equal rights (as opposed to special rights). Notice, then, that this analysis relies on cases such as *Moreno* and *Cleburne*, and is not analytically the same as *Brown* and *Loving*, which hold that hierarchy is by itself objectionable, no matter what the state's purpose. The illegitimate purpose animating the classification is, it seems, a key to showing that, despite appearances, the law in *Romer* does not bear a rational relationship to a legitimate governmental interest.

CFV greeted the opinion with strident denunciation. Will Perkins described the forces that had prevailed as "forces bent on forcing a deviant life style down the throats of the American people."[20] He called the ruling "truly a chilling day for people of conscience across America." He opined that Americans would soon rise up to impeach the six justices who had joined the majority opinion.[21]

In *Romer* Justice Kennedy was on secure ground. From the first to the last, illegitimate intent was written all over the law and its defense. For this very reason, however, *Romer* is a narrow holding, which offers little guidance for future antidiscrimination cases involving sexual orientation. When illegitimate intent can be plainly found, a law imposing disadvantages on gays and lesbians will be found to lack a rational basis. Rational basis review might certainly be extended in a tough-minded way to invalidate other forms of discrimination against gays and lesbians. But what about more subtle disadvantages, or more narrowly drawn disqualifications? Such laws might well survive rational basis review. The question of heightened scrutiny, therefore, remains central. The secure protection of gays and lesbians from a wide variety of disadvantages would seem to require a holding that laws involving that classification, like laws involving race or gender, warrant some form of heightened scrutiny.

5. SUSPECT CLASSIFICATION: SEX DISCRIMINATION? IMMUTABILITY?

One route to heightened scrutiny was explored by the Colorado Supreme Court. This fundamental rights approach, however, is hard to justify in terms of the precedents and useful only in a narrow range of cases, those involving laws imposing broad-based disadvantages in the political process.

The suspect classification approach is thus to be preferred. But there are two interestingly different versions of that approach, and we must now ask which is the more promising.

First is what we may call the straightforward approach: argue that sexual orientation is, in and of itself, a suspect classification. This approach has a lot going for it, given that gays and lesbians can point to such a long and ugly history of discrimination. It has, however, repeatedly failed, because courts have been unwilling to grant that the traditional criteria of suspectness are present.

Some theorists have therefore tried out a different approach, the sex equality approach. Classifications involving sex already get intermediate scrutiny: so this approach is an attempt to include protection for gays and lesbians in this already recognized legal category. Here's how this approach goes, as defended by Andrew Koppelman, its most eloquent and tenacious advocate.

Consider antimiscegenation laws: What tells us that these laws involve a racial classification is that if you change the race of one of the parties, the proposed union is permissible. Suppose John is black and Sally is white: they can't get married under such laws. But substitute Mary for Sally—and Mary happens to be black—and, lo and behold, John and Mary can get married. So, the classification is a suspect one, based on race. Similarly, let's take Jennifer and Susan. Jennifer and Susan live in a state that forbids adoption by same-sex couples, so they can't adopt a child. (I'm deliberately deferring, here, the difficult issue of same-sex marriage.) But just change Susan to Bob, and Bob happens to be male, and, lo and behold, the disability goes away: the change from one sex to another makes all the difference. Notice that we haven't even mentioned orientation: the point is that wherever a change of a male to a female or a female to a male makes a decisive legal difference, that law involves a classification based upon sex, and such classifications deserve heightened scrutiny.

This is a clever argument, but to many people it seems legalistic in the pejorative sense: that is, it finds a loophole, but it doesn't quite get at what is really going on. What's really going on when a disability is imposed on Jennifer and Susan is that the nature of their sexual orientation is being penalized. People think that their sexuality is bad, and they want to prevent children from growing up in that "pathological" atmosphere. The right way of thinking about the classification is that it involves sexual orientation, and it's really not discrimination against women as such. There is an analogy to the miscegenation laws, to be sure, but it is superficial: the argument doesn't reach deeply enough to get at the real source of the discrimination.

At this point, however, Koppelman has a fascinating reply. Look deeply into prejudice against homosexuals as such and you will find that indeed, at its root, it is all about sex discrimination: it's a way of maintaining binary divisions of the sexes and the patriarchal control of men over women. What is troubling about Jennifer and Susan is that they have been able to evade this patriarchal control. So in a deep as well as a superficial sense, the discrimination they face is a form of sex discrimination.

Well, that's probably true—of a lot of prejudice against lesbians. Maybe such thinking even plays some part in explaining prejudice against gay men: Oscar Wilde's refusal of his patriarchal role, his choice of sex for pleasure, shocked the British. Perhaps in some instances prejudice against gay men takes the more general form of anxiety at the way in which their relationships confound gender distinctions. But prejudice against gay men—which is really what drives antigay efforts in America—taps, as well, and more centrally, profound anxieties about bodily penetrability and vulnerability (anxieties that are felt, above all, by men). Those deep bodily anxieties cannot be explained in terms of a fear of losing control over women. The fact that the antigay movement has from its inception almost totally ignored lesbians is difficult to reconcile with Koppelman's deeper thesis.

So I conclude (though with enormous respect for Koppelman's important work) that this thesis, although it indeed does identify one part of what is going on in discrimination against gays and lesbians,[22] is seriously incomplete and therefore is not the most satisfactory way to get heightened protection for gays and lesbians under the Equal Protection Clause. We are back, then, to the straightforward approach. What argument might lead to its acceptance by courts?

We begin by noting that the traditional indicia of heightened scrutiny—history of discrimination, political powerlessness, and immutability—are indicia, not necessary conditions. They emerged gradually over time, and they have been found useful in a range of cases, but the Court has never held that all three have to be present.

Next, we should try to get at the intuitive idea behind these indicia. A key idea seems to be: when a group is so placed in society that there's a good bet that classifications involving that group will be in some way tainted by prejudice, we need to look more closely. Notice that this worry about prejudice is considerably broader than *Romer*'s worry about animus. When a group has experienced a history of prejudice, often involving stereotyping, classifications involving that group may be tainted by those stereotypes even when nobody has malicious intentions toward the group. Classifications involving women, particularly, are likely to be prejudicial, relying on demeaning stereotypes, even without animus. As Justice Brennan wrote in *Frontiero v. Richardson*, the case that established heightened scrutiny for gender-based classifications:

> There can be no doubt that our Nation has had a long and unfortunate history of sex discrimination. Traditionally, such discrimination was rationalized by an attitude of "romantic paternalism" which, in practical effect, put women, not on a pedestal, but in a cage.... As a result... our statute books gradually became laden with gross, stereotyped distinctions between the sexes.[23]

Heightened scrutiny is warranted not because of malicious intent (after all, "romantic paternalism" was intended to be benign), but because of a history of deformed views of women that impede their full equality.

So it's the history of discrimination that makes us worry about such classifications, lest they be infected that way. That, I suggest, is and should be the central criterion of suspectness, the one that goes to the heart of why heightened scrutiny is felt to be needed in certain cases.

Political powerlessness is important, when it is, because of the history of discrimination: where there is a lot of prejudice, a group probably doesn't have much opportunity to influence legislators to take its own interests seriously, and of course that would give us a reason to be suspicious of classifications disadvantaging that group. As Justice Brennan wrote in a 1985 case, "Because of the immediate and severe opprobrium often manifested against homosexuals once so identified publicly, members of this group are particularly powerless to pursue their rights openly in the political arena."[24] If the key notion is that of prejudice-infected classification, however, we should not say that political powerlessness is a necessary condition of heightened scrutiny. Some groups might have done a lot of political mobilization and still be the targets of overwhelming prejudice and stereotyping. This is clearly true of women, even today. People with disabilities have organizations defending their interests, and they have been able to enact laws in their own interest; and yet, evidence of continuing discrimination against them is so strong that the case for some form of heightened scrutiny is strong. Gays and lesbians are in a similar situation: although they have been able to organize and engage in political action, there is still overwhelming prejudice and stigma associated with the classification, so the fact that such political action exists should not debar them from a form of heightened scrutiny.

What about immutability? This criterion has frequently been challenged, and we can see why. Suppose it were possible to take a pill and change one's race: does that make race-based discrimination less problematic? People can and do change their sex, but that does not alter the case for heightened scrutiny, given the history of discrimination against women. And of course religion is fully chosen and mutable, but that doesn't make us think any better of religion-based discrimination. (Of course religion, being protected under the First Amendment, does not figure in the traditional enumeration of equal protection categories, but the idea is what counts here.) So it might seem irrelevant whether sexual orientation is genetic or acquired during early childhood (probably some combination of both is the right answer), or even formed later on.

Let's try to get at the idea underlying legal reference to immutability by looking at a key text: again, it is Justice Brennan's plurality
opinion in *Frontiero*:

> Moreover, since sex, like race and national origin, is an immu-
> table characteristic determined solely by the accident of birth,
> the imposition of special disabilities upon the members of a
> particular sex because of their sex would seem to violate "the
> basic concept of our system that legal burdens should bear some
> relationship to individual responsibility." And what differenti-
> ates sex from such nonsuspect statuses as intelligence or phys-
> ical disability, and aligns it with the recognized suspect criteria,
> is that the sex characteristic frequently bears no relation to
> ability to perform or contribute to society. As a result, statutory
> distinctions between the sexes often have the effect of invidi-
> ously relegating the entire class of females to inferior legal status
> without regard to the actual capabilities of its individual
> members.

This paragraph makes it clear that what is really at issue is not
immutability as such, but irrelevance to the purpose at hand. Justice
Brennan expresses no view about whether intelligence is hereditary,
and wisely too: nobody has yet managed to sort out the different
environmental and hereditary factors contributing to intelligence,
and we permissibly make intelligence relevant to employment
without settling that question. In some cases—for example, musical
ability—we have a pretty good idea that the basis of the ability is
inherited and in that sense immutable—and yet we do not tell
symphony orchestras that they may not hire people based on musical
ability. The crucial thought has nothing to do with immutability as
such; the thought is that women have for centuries been stereo-
typed as incapable in virtue of being women, without examining

the characteristics of an individual that may be relevant to a given job. That is why those classifications are suspect. They take one time-honored status, with which lots of stereotypes are associated, and they infer from it other characteristics, which may or may not follow, rather than focusing on the properties that are pertinent to the job at hand. The immutability of the status figures, here, as a reason why it has endured through time, in such a way that many stereotypes have grown up around it. But the key factor that makes the classification suspect is its irrelevance.

Let's now return to sexual orientation. The right way to think about that case in the light of *Frontiero* is to think of the many ways in which stereotypes of gays and lesbians cause people to ascribe to them all sorts of characteristics that make it seem acceptable to treat them badly. For example, gays and lesbians are often excluded from jobs involving teaching because of the stereotype of the gay or lesbian person as child molester. This stereotype is itself unsupported by evidence, and it leads to all sorts of unfair judgments about individuals. Instead, hiring institutions should examine the background of the individual (whether heterosexual or homosexual), asking whether anything gives reason for suspicion about that person's behavior with the young. The analogy with *Frontiero* is strong, and it is not about immutability as such. Immutability is relevant to the extent that the classification has endured over time and many prejudices have sprung up around it. But the key notion is the irrelevance of the status to the purposes for which (driven by prejudice) people use it.

There's another very different thought that immutability also introduces: the idea of depth and centrality in someone's way of life. Why is it that believing that sexual orientation is innate sometimes causes people to be more sympathetic to gays and lesbians, more willing to oppose prejudice against them? I think the connection goes like this. We used to think that being gay or lesbian was an unwise choice, like smoking. Admittedly, such chosen behaviors can be difficult to change, as smoking surely is, but we think it's reasonable to pass laws disadvantaging smokers, because we think that smokers can learn to restrain themselves, or to change. Of course smoking harms nonconsenting parties and homosexuality does not (or does so, like heterosexuality, only when someone engages in nonconsensual behavior). So the analogy is far from perfect. The person who thought that homosexuality was like smoking should think again! Still, let's now imagine such a person learning that homosexual orientation is either based in the genes or fixed in very early childhood, or some combination of the two. Now the person is likely to think differently: we can hardly expect people to change, if that's how it is. So it seems punitive to pass laws disadvantaging people for what they can't help about themselves.

However, that thought remains incomplete without a further thought: sex is central to the pursuit of happiness. Suppose we discovered that some people have a genetically based orientation that makes them more likely than others to prefer risky behavior. We would not necessarily feel (I think) that we should drop laws that limit the risks people may run in ways that do not impinge on the well-being of others (such as laws requiring motorcycle helmets). Some will support such laws and others will consider them intrusive or silly. But they don't seem to raise fundamental liberty issues. The difference is that we just don't believe that riding a motorcycle without a helmet is central to the meaning of life. We are not crippling people's personalities by asking them to wear a helmet. Sexual orientation, by contrast, seems to lie deep in the structure of people's personalities, in ways that are crucial to their pursuit of happiness. Therefore, to ask people to change in that respect, or not to express their orientation, is to impose a very crippling burden. In estimating the costs imposed, we naturally ask what alternatives the person has, and here the idea that the orientation in question is set very early and is difficult to change becomes significant. But the main idea is one of depth and importance. (As we shall see in chapter 5, the Iowa Supreme Court makes this point well.)

Once again, this reasoning does not really concern immutability—for we already saw in chapter 2 that we reason in a very similar way about religion, which is intimate and central, but not immutable. Perhaps a little extra work is done by *immutability*, in reminding us of how punitive it is to disadvantage people (in a matter central to the meaning of life) when they can't change.

So the legal notion of immutability is confused, but it leads us to two good ideas, both pertinent to our question: the idea of relevance and the idea of depth or centrality. With respect to both of those ideas, the case for heightened scrutiny for sexual orientation is very strong. Sexual orientation, like being female, is irrelevant to many things for which society confusedly holds it to be relevant. It is also deep and central in people's lives, like religion, in a way that makes us think asking people to give up acting on their orientation is a kind of cruelty.

Judges are understandably reluctant to multiply the number of classifications that get heightened scrutiny. One benefit of looking in such detail at the history of Amendment 2, however, is that it tells us how extensive the record of discrimination against gays and lesbians actually is. In that case, the law did not even pass rational basis review because of the overwhelming evidence of illicit intent. In many other cases, however, the history of discrimination and the pervasiveness of the stereotype, rather than malicious intent, influence the classification; people may just be going along with historical stereotypes rather than having animus against the group in question. To root out discrimination in such cases, we need heightened scrutiny.

Romer shows us a lot about how majority social attitudes put pressure on minorities. Amendment 2 was a classic example of Devlinesque politics: the indignation and disgust of the average person enabled the law, and a vulnerable minority was deprived, in a sweeping way, of privileges and entitlements that are the ordinary stuff of democratic politics. The result in *Romer*, like the result in *Lawrence*, was a victory for the "politics of humanity," a politics based on equal respect and on an attempt to move beyond stereotypes to an honest confrontation with the real lives of the group and its members. It was also, in a closely connected way, a victory for the general approach to politics mapped out by John Stuart Mill, one in which majority attitudes are not allowed to deprive minorities of equal rights.

Romer was a narrow result. Much remains to be done to get clear about what is and is not permissible in this area. Judges can and should contribute to this progress: as I've argued, the narrow notion of animus needs to be extended by the development of a clearly defined idea of heightened scrutiny. Good legislation, however, is also essential. Many states and municipalities have antidiscrimination laws for sexual orientation, but the United States as such has none, and too few political resources have been devoted to the effort to enact one. Many Americans who abhor the idea of same-sex marriage are ready to grant that gays and lesbians should be protected from discrimination in housing, employment, and other areas of daily life. It is a pity that women and people with disabilities enjoy such protections at the federal level while gays and lesbians do not.

Romer was, however, a decisive moment. Rarely had disgust been so openly on display in a Supreme Court case, and rarely has the Court rejected its politics so plainly.

NOTES

1. Significantly, the website highlights interracial families: CFV has always tried to make common cause with groups representing the interests of racial minorities, as the campaign for Amendment 2 shows.

2. *Romer v. Evans*, 517 U.S. 620 (1996). The Denver ordinances date from 1991, Boulder's from 1987, and Aspen's from 1977.

3. Although Romer is named as chief litigant during all phases of the Amendment 2 struggle, he opposed the referendum and remained personally committed to nondiscrimination.

4. Joyce Murdoch and Deb Price, *Courting Justice: Gay Men and Lesbians v. the Supreme Court* (New York: Basic Books, 2002), 452.

5. Ibid.

6. Ibid.

7. *Corporation of Presiding Bishop v. Amos*, 483 U.S. 327 (1987).

8. CFV pamphlet: *Equal Rights Not Special Rights*.

9. *Evans v. Romer*, 854 P.2d 1270 (Colo.); affirmed on other grounds, 517 U.S. 620 (1993, henceforth, Evans 1). Initially Judge Bayless argued that public law may not "endorse and give effect to private biases," citing *Palmore v. Sidoti*, 466 U.S. 429 (1984), a custody case concerning a divorced mother who had remarried, to an African-American man; the ex-husband sought to remove custody, on the ground that the child would suffer from social prejudice. This case, however, was not helpful to the plaintiffs, since it involved a race-based classification, which already gave a secure rationale for heightened scrutiny. For good reason, the Colorado Supreme Court sought a strategy that would hook the case at hand more securely into traditional equal protection arguments for heightened scrutiny.

10. This was the central argument given by the dissenting opinion for rejecting the analysis of the majority.

11. *Evans v. Romer*, 1993 WL 518586 (Colo. Dist. Ct.).

12. See http://www.qrd.org/qrd/usa/colorado/1994/norton.paid.paul.cameron. big.bucks-outfront-08.14.94. Although this particular story is from a gay-friendly publication, it's clear that Norton publicly admitted to paying Cameron, and admitted to the amount of $10,125. There may have been other payments; Norton's office never cooperated fully with the press, and revealed that amount only when the reporter said he'd use the state law's freedom-of-information provision to force disclosure. Norton, then running

for reelection, preferred to concede the $10,000 rather than to face a full-scale inquiry.

13. One of the more famous such witnesses was Charles Socarides, Freudian analyst and practitioner of "conversion therapy" for homosexuality. Socarides was never expelled from the American Psychoanalytical Association, but he was denounced by the association for representing his own views as association views, and threatened with legal action should he continue to do so.

14. Novak later joined forces with me and other scholars on both sides of the issue to sponsor a serious academic conference on the topic of homosexuality and rights that generated a useful book: *Sexual Orientation and Human Rights in American Religious Discourse*, ed. Saul M. Olyan and Martha Nussbaum (New York: Oxford University Press, 1998).

15. Deposition of Harvey Mansfield, October 8, 1993. (A deposition is sworn testimony.)

16. 882 P.2d 1335: 1994 Colo. (hereafter *Evans* 2).

17. 413 U.S. 528 (1973). Because *Moreno* concerned a federal, not a state, program, it was argued with reference to the Equal Protection Clause of the Fifth, not the Fourteenth Amendment.

18. Ibid. at 534.

19. See particularly Andrew Koppelman, *"Romer v. Evans* and Invidious Intent," *William and Mary Bill of Rights Journal* 6 (1997), 89–146.

20. David W. Dunlap, "The Gay Rights Ruling: In Colorado, Ruling Signals More Fights to Come," *New York Times*, May 21, 1996.

21. Ibid.

22. Koppelman concedes that it does not capture some of the most serious wrongs, in "Defending the Sex Discrimination Argument for Lesbian and Gay Rights: A Reply to Edward Stein," *UCLA Law Review* 49 (2001), 519–38.

23. *Frontiero v. Richardson*, 411 U.S. 677 (1973).

24. *Rowland v. Mad River Local School District*, 470 U.S. 1009 (1985).

CHAPTER FIVE

A Right to Marry?

The freedom to marry has long been recognized as one of the vital personal rights essential to the orderly pursuit of happiness by free men.

U.S. SUPREME COURT, *LOVING V. VIRGINIA* (1967)

[T]here are many persons for whom it is not enough that the inequality has no just or legitimate defence; they require to be told what express advantage would be obtained by abolishing it.

To which let me first answer, the advantage of having the most universal and pervading of all human relations regulated by justice instead of injustice.

—JOHN STUART MILL,
THE SUBJECTION OF WOMEN[1]

I. WHAT IS MARRIAGE?

Marriage is both ubiquitous and central. All across our country, in every region, every social class, every race and ethnicity, every religion or nonreligion, people get married. For many if not most people, moreover, marriage is not a trivial matter. It is a key to the pursuit of happiness, something people aspire to—and keep on aspiring to, again and again, even when their experience has been far from happy. To be told, "You cannot get married" is thus to be excluded from one of the defining rituals of the American life cycle.

The keys to the kingdom of the married might have been held only by private citizens—religious bodies and their leaders, families, other parts of civil society. So it has been in many societies throughout history. In the United States, however, as in most modern nations, government currently holds those keys. Even if people have been married by their church or religious group, they are not married in the sense that really counts for social and political purposes unless they have been granted a marriage license by the state. Unlike private actors, however, the state doesn't have complete freedom to decide who may and may not marry. The state's involvement raises fundamental issues about equality of political and civic standing.

Same-sex marriage is currently one of the most divisive political issues in our nation. In November 2008, Californians passed Proposition 8, a referendum that removed the right to marry from same-sex couples who had been granted that right by the courts. That same day, California voters passed sweeping legislation protecting animals from cruelty in the factory farming industry—thus showing that they are neither rigid traditionalists nor indifferent to suffering. And yet, a majority saw fit to deny some of their fellow citizens a fundamental right, in a way that was felt by the same-sex community as deeply degrading and humiliating. In May, the California Supreme

Court upheld the referendum, although it did not annul the marriages that had been legally performed before it. The whole question is bound to come before voters again soon. Analyzing this issue may help us understand what is happening in our country, and where we may be able to go from here.

Before we approach the issue of same-sex marriage, we must define marriage. But marriage, it soon becomes evident, is no single thing. It is plural in both content and meaning. The institution of marriage houses and supports several distinct aspects of human life: sexual relations, friendship and companionship, love, conversation, procreation and child rearing, mutual responsibility. Marriages can exist without each of these. (We have always granted marriage licenses to sterile people, people too old to have children, irresponsible people, and people incapable of love and friendship. Impotence, lack of interest in sex, and refusal to allow intercourse may count as grounds of divorce, but they don't preclude marriage.) Marriages can exist even in cases where none of these is present, though such marriages are probably unhappy. Each of these important aspects of human life, in turn, can exist outside of marriage, and they can even exist all together outside of marriage, as is evident from the fact that many unmarried couples live lives of intimacy, friendship, and mutual responsibility, and have and raise children (though these children, deemed illegitimate, used to suffer social and legal disadvantages). Nonetheless, when people ask themselves what the content of marriage is, they typically think of this cluster of things.

Nor is the meaning of marriage single. Marriage has, first, a civil rights aspect. Married people get a lot of government benefits that the unmarried usually do not get: favorable treatment in tax, inheritance, and insurance status; immigration rights; rights in adoption and custody; decisional and visitation rights in health care and burial; the spousal privilege exemption when giving testimony in court; and yet others.

Marriage has, second, an expressive aspect. When people get married, they typically make a statement of love and commitment in front of witnesses. Most people who get married view that statement as a very important part of their lives. Being able to make it, and to make it freely (not under duress) is taken to be definitive of adult human freedom. The statement made by the marrying couple is usually seen as involving an answering statement on the part of society: we declare our love and commitment, and society, in response, recognizes and dignifies that commitment.

Marriage has, finally, a religious aspect. For many people, a marriage is not complete unless it has been solemnized by the relevant authorities in their religion, according to the rules of the religion.

Despite the fact that marriage has these three aspects, government currently plays a key role in all. It confers and administers benefits. It seems, at least, to operate as an agent of recognition or the granting of dignity. And it forms alliances with religious bodies. Clergy are always among those entitled to perform legally binding marriages. Religions may refuse to marry people who are eligible for state marriage, and they may also agree to marry people who are ineligible for state marriage. But much of the officially sanctioned marrying currently done in the United States is done on religious premises by religious personnel. What they are solemnizing (when there is a license granted by the state) is, however, not only a religious ritual, but also a public rite of passage—the entry into a privileged civic status.

To get this privileged treatment under law people do not have to show that they are good people. Convicted felons, divorced parents who fail to pay child support, people with a record of domestic violence or emotional abuse, delinquent taxpayers, drug abusers, rapists, murderers, racists, anti-Semites, other bigots, all can marry if they choose, and indeed are held to have a fundamental constitutional right to do so[2]—so long as they want to marry someone of the opposite sex. Although some religions urge premarital counseling and refuse to marry people who seem ill prepared for marriage, the state does not turn such people away. The most casual whim may become a marriage with no impediment other than the time it takes to get a license. Moreover, the rules about who gets to perform a marriage impose no impediment. One may become ordained over the internet as a minister of the Universal Life Church or some other internet-based religion. Some states encourage friends to perform marriages by permitting any person to do so a maximum of once a year.

Nor do people even have to lead a sexual lifestyle of the type the majority prefers in order to get married. Pedophiles, sadists, masochists, sodomites, transsexuals—all can get married by the state, so long as they marry someone of the opposite sex.

Given all this, it seems odd to suggest that in marrying people the state affirmatively expresses its approval, or confers dignity. There is indeed something odd about the mixture of casualness and solemnity with which the state behaves as a marrying agent. Nonetheless, it seems to most people that the state, by giving a marriage license, expresses approval and, by withholding it, disapproval.

What is the same-sex marriage debate about? It is really not about whether same-sex relationships can involve the content of marriage: few would deny that gays and lesbians are capable of friendship, intimacy, "meet and happy conversation," and mutual responsibility, nor that they can have and raise children (whether their own from a previous marriage, children created within their relationship by surrogacy or artificial insemination, or adopted children). Certainly none would deny that gays and lesbians are capable of sexual intimacy, because that is typically the focus of animus toward same-sex relationships.

Nor is the debate, at least currently, about the civil aspects of marriage: we are moving toward a consensus that same-sex couples and opposite-sex couples ought to enjoy equal civil rights. The leaders of both major political parties appeared to endorse this position during the 2008 presidential campaign, although not all Republicans have fully endorsed a regime of civil unions and thus far only a handful of states have legalized civil unions with material privileges equivalent to those of marriage. (As I shall shortly discuss, however, the Defense of Marriage Act means that no unions or marriages for same-sex couples are fully equal materially to opposite-sex marriage.)

Finally, the debate is not about the religious aspects of marriage. Most of the major religions have their own internal debates, frequently heated, over the status of same-sex unions. Some denominations—Unitarian Universalism and Reform and Conservative Judaism—have endorsed marriage for same-sex couples. Others, such as the Protestant Episcopal Church of the United States, have taken a friendly position toward these unions. Presbyterians, Lutherans, and Methodists are divided on the issue at present, and American Roman Catholics, both lay and clergy, are divided, although the church hierarchy is strongly opposed. Still other religions (Southern Baptists, the Church of Jesus Christ of Latter-Day Saints) seem strongly opposed as a body to the recognition of such unions. There is no single religious position on these unions in America today, but the heat of those debates is, typically, internal and denominational; it is not that heat that spills over into the public realm. Under any state of the law, moreover, particular religions would be free to marry or not to marry same-sex couples.

The public debate, instead, is primarily about marriage's expressive aspects. It is here that the difference between civil unions and marriage resides, and it is this aspect that is at issue when same-sex couples reject the compromise offer of civil unions, demanding nothing less than marriage. It is because marriage is taken to confer some kind of dignity or public approval on the parties and their union that the exclusion of gays and lesbians from marriage is seen (even when they are entitled to civil unions conferring the benefits of marriage) as stigmatizing and degrading, raising issues of equal civic standing and equal protection of the laws.

The expressive dimension of marriage raises several distinct questions. First, assuming that granting a marriage license expresses a type of public approval, should the state be in the business of expressing favor for, or dignifying, some unions rather than others? In other words, are there any good public reasons for the state to be in the marriage business at all, rather than the civil union business? Second, if there are such good reasons, what are the arguments for and against admitting same-sex couples to that status, and how should we think about them?

It is very important to keep these two questions distinct. It is possible to argue, and I shall argue, that, so long as the state is in the marrying business, equality concerns require it to offer marriage to same-sex couples—but that it would be a lot better, as a matter of both political theory and public policy, if the state withdrew from the marrying business, leaving the expressive domain to the religions and to other private groups with which people may associate themselves, and offering civil unions to both same- and opposite-sex couples.

In what follows, an important point about federalism must be borne in mind. No state on its own may create unions for gays and lesbians, whether called "civil unions" or "marriages," that are fully equal to the opposite-sex marriages, because the federal Defense of Marriage Act announces that other states are not required to recognize these unions and they will not be recognized by the federal government. This is both a material and an expressive problem. The Defense of Marriage Act is still being defended by the Justice Department in the Obama administration, despite Obama's campaign statement that he would seek its repeal.

2. MARRIAGE IN HISTORY: THE MYTH OF THE GOLDEN AGE

When people talk about the institution of marriage these days, they often wax nostalgic. Until very recently, they think and often say, marriage used to be a lifelong commitment by one man and one woman, sanctified by God and the state, for the purposes of companionship and the rearing of children. People lived by those rules and were happy. Typical, if somewhat rhetorical, is this statement by Senator Robert Byrd of West Virginia during the debates over the Defense of Marriage Act:

> Mr. President, throughout the annals of human experience, in dozens of civilizations and cultures of varying value systems, humanity has discovered that the permanent relationship between men and women is a keystone to the stability, strength, and health of human society—a relationship worthy of legal recognition and judicial protection.

We used to live in that golden age of marital purity, the story goes. Now, however, things are falling apart. Divorce is ubiquitous. Children are growing up without sufficient guidance, support, and love, as adults live for selfish pleasure alone. We need to come to our senses and return to the rules that used to make us all happy.

Like most Golden Age myths, this one contains a core of truth: commitment and responsibility are under strain in our culture, and too many children are indeed growing up without enough economic or emotional support. We can't think well about how to solve this problem, however, unless we first recognize the flaws in this mythic depiction of our own past. Like all fantasies of purity, this one masks a reality that is far more varied, complex, and, often, troubled.

To begin with, Senator Byrd's idea that lifelong monogamous marriage has been the norm throughout human history is just mistaken. Many societies have embraced various forms of polygamy, informal or common-law marriage, and sequential monogamy. People who based their ethical norms on the Bible too rarely take note of the fact that the society depicted in the Old Testament is polygamous. Numerous patriarchs are depicted as having plural wives, and many also had socially approved concubines. Even the wording of the Ten Commandments in their second occurrence in *Deuteronomy* (5:1–18) presupposes polygamy: the commandment not to covet a neighbor's spouse is addressed only to men, whereas the commandment not to covet the neighbor's house, goods, and so on is addressed to both men and women; an unmarried woman could covet another woman's husband (commentaries point out), because she could become that man's additional wife.

In many other ancient societies (and some modern ones) sex outside marriage was or is a routine matter: in ancient Greece, for example, married men routinely had socially approved sexual relationships with prostitutes (male and female), and, with some restrictions, with younger male citizens. One reason for this custom was that women were secluded and uneducated, thus not able to share a male's political and intellectual aspirations. People in many times and places have linked erotic desire to friendship and shared pursuits.

If we turn to Republican Rome, a society more like our own in basing marriage on an ideal of love and companionship,[3] we find that this very ideal gave rise to widespread divorce, as both women and men sought a partner with whom they could be happy and share a common life. We hardly find a major Roman figure, male or female, who did not marry at least twice. Moreover, Roman marriages were typically not monogamous on the side of the male, who was expected to have sexual relations with both males and females of lower status (slaves, prostitutes); even if wives at times protested, they understood the practice as typical and ubiquitous.[4] These Romans are often admired (and rightly so, I think) as good citizens, people who believed in civic virtue and tried hard to run a government based on that commitment. Certainly for the founders of the United States the Roman Republic was a key source of both political norms and personal heroes. And yet these heroes did not live in a marital Eden.

In fact, there is no better antidote to the myth of marital purity than to read Cicero's account of the unhappy marriage of his brother Quintus to Pomponia Attica, the sister of his best friend Atticus. Through his narrative (however biased in his brother's favor) we get a glimpse of something so familiar that it is difficult to believe that it all happened around 50 BCE. Cicero is out in the country on one of his estates, and his brother has (it seems) dragged his unwilling wife away from the city to spend a week on the farm—with a brother-in-law who doesn't like her and who, despite his undoubted greatness, is more than a little self-obsessed:

> When we arrived there Quintus said in the kindest way, "Pomponia, will you ask the women in, and I'll get the boys?" Both what he said and his intention and manner were perfectly pleasant, at least it seemed so to me. Pomponia however answered in our hearing, "I am a guest here myself."...Quintus said to me, "There! This is the sort of thing I have to put up with every day."...I myself was quite shocked. Her words and manner were so gratuitously rude. [They all go in to lunch, except for Pomponia, who goes straight to her room; Quintus has some food sent up to her, which she refuses.] In a word, I felt my brother could not have been more forbearing nor your sister ruder. And I have left out a number of things that annoyed me at the time more than they did Quintus. [The following day, Quintus has a

talk with his brother.] He told me that Pomponia had refused to sleep with him, and that her attitude when he left the house was just as I had seen it the day before. Well, you can tell her for me that her whole conduct was lacking in sympathy.[5]

(The marriage lasted six more unhappy years and then ended in divorce.)

Often we dismiss the customs of ancient times (e.g., biblical polygamy) as so distant from our own that no comparison makes sense. The shock of seeing our own face in the mirror of Cicero's intimate narrative reminds us that human beings always have a hard time sustaining love and even friendship, that bad temper, incompatibility, and divergent desires are no invention of the sexual revolution. Certainly they are not caused by the recognition of same-sex marriage. We've always lived in a postlapsarian world.

The rise of divorce in the modern era, moreover, was spurred not by a hatred of marriage, but, far more, by a high conception of what marriage ought to be. It's not just that people began to think that women had a right to divorce on grounds of bodily cruelty, and that divorce of that sort was a good thing. It's also that Christians began insisting—just like those ancient Romans—that marriage was about much more than procreation and sexual relations. John Milton's famous defense of divorce on grounds of incompatibility emphasizes "meet and happy conversation" as the central goal of marriage, and notes that marriage ought to fulfill not simply bodily drives, but also the "intellectual and innocent desire" that leads people to want to talk a lot to each other. People are entitled to demand this from their marriages, he argues, and entitled to divorce if they do not find it. If we adopt Milton's attractive view, we should not see divorce as expressing (necessarily) a falling away from high moral ideals, but rather as expressing an unwillingness to put up with a relationship that does not fulfill, or at least seriously pursue, high ideals.

In our own nation, as historians of marriage emphasize, a social norm of monogamous marriage was salient, from colonial times onward.[6] The norm, however, like most norms in all times and places, was not the same as the reality. Studying the reality of marital discord and separation is very difficult, because many if not most broken marriages were not formally terminated by divorce. Given that until rather recently divorce was hard to obtain, and given that America offered so much space for relocation and the reinvention of self, many individuals, both male and female, simply moved away and started life somewhere else. A man who showed up with a "wife" in tow was not likely to encounter a background check to find out whether he had ever been legally divorced from a former spouse; such background checks across state lines would have been virtually impossible. A woman who showed up calling herself "the Widow Jones" would not be asked to show her husband's death certificate before she could form a new relationship and marry. Men left for the West during the Gold Rush and didn't return. Women moved to cities and set up boardinghouses, or took jobs in factories. The cases of separation and attempted remarriage that do end up in court are the tip of a vast uncharted iceberg. If, as historian Hendrik Hartog concludes about the nineteenth century, "Marital mobility marked American legal and constitutional life,"[7] it marked, far more, the daily lives of Americans who did not litigate their separations.

One vivid example of this daily reality is the life of Andrew Jackson's wife, Rachel. She and her first husband separated; they moved to different states. She met Jackson and married him—but she was still legally married to someone else. Because she "married" a man soon to be famous, her story ended up in the news. If she hadn't been with a famous man, nobody would have noticed.

Insofar as monogamy was reality, we should never forget that it rested on the disenfranchisement of women. Indeed, the rise of divorce in recent years is probably connected to women's social and political empowerment, more than to any other single factor. When women had no rights, no marketable skills, and hence no exit options, they often had to put up with bad marriages, with adultery, neglect, even with domestic violence. When women are able to leave, many demand a better deal. This simple economic explanation for the rise of divorce—combined with Milton's emphasis on people's need for emotional attunement and conversation—is much more powerful than the idea of a fall from ethical purity in explaining how we've moved from where we were to where we are today. But if such factors are salient, denial of marriage to same-sex couples is hardly the way to address them.

Throughout the nineteenth and early twentieth centuries, a distinctive feature of American marriage has been the strategic use of federalism. Marriage laws have always been state laws (despite recurrent attempts to legislate a national law of marriage and divorce[8]). But states in the United States have typically used that power to compete with one another, and marriage quickly became a scene of competition. Long before Nevada became famous as a divorce haven, with its short residency requirement, other states assumed that role. For quite a stretch of time, Indiana (surprisingly) was the divorce haven for couples fleeing the strict requirements of states such as New York (one of the strictest until extremely recently) and Wisconsin. Other havens at various times were Connecticut and South Dakota. The reasons a state liberalized its laws were complex, but at least some of them were economic: while couples lived out the residency requirement, they would spend money in the state.[9] Other states kept their laws strict to attract another group of citizens. In short, marriage laws "became public packages of goods and services that competed against the public goods of other jurisdictions for the loyalty and the tax dollars of a mobile citizenry."[10]

What we're seeing today, as seven states (Massachusetts, Connecticut, Iowa, Maine, New Hampshire, Vermont, and, briefly, California) have legalized same-sex marriage, as others (California, Vermont, until September 2009, and Connecticut before the recent court decision) have offered civil unions with marriagelike benefits, and yet others (New York) have announced that, although they will not perform same-sex marriages themselves, they will recognize those legally contracted in other jurisdictions, is the same sort of competitive process—with, however, one important difference. The federal Defense of Marriage Act has made it clear that states need not give legal recognition to marriages legally contracted elsewhere. That was not the case with competing divorce regimes: once legally divorced in some other U.S. state, the parties were considered divorced in their own state as well.

The anomalous situation of same-sex marriage—in which a couple may be legally married in one state or a group of states, but unmarried in another—has given rise to a host of legal quandaries. Suppose David and Larry marry in Massachusetts. Larry then goes on a business trip to Chicago and falls gravely ill there. Does David have the right to make critical medical decisions about his care? Suppose, instead, David goes to Texas and is arrested for a crime there. Larry is served a subpoena to testify to crucial information he is thought to possess. Does Larry have the right to refuse to testify on grounds of spousal immunity? These and countless other conflict-of-laws issues await resolution.[11] Federalism encourages experimentation. In the absence of mutual recognition, however, it leaves the law with a long and difficult agenda.

Although the situation of nonrecognition faced by same-sex couples does not parallel the history of our varying divorce regimes, it does have a major historical precedent. States that had laws against miscegenation refused to recognize marriages between blacks and whites legally contracted elsewhere, and even criminalized those marriages. The Supreme Court case that brought about the overturning of the antimiscegenation laws, *Loving v. Virginia*, was such a case. Mildred Jeter (African-American) and Richard Loving (white) got married in Washington, D.C., in 1958. Their marriage was not recognized as legal in their home state of Virginia. When they returned there they were arrested in the middle of the night in their own bedroom.[12] Their marriage certificate was hanging on the wall over their bed. The state prosecuted them, since interracial marriage was a felony in Virginia, and they were convicted. The judge then told them either to leave the state for twenty-five years or to spend one year in jail. They left, but began the litigation that led to the landmark 1967 decision.

Richard Loving was killed in a car accident in 1975; Mildred survived until May 2008. Looking back at her case on its fortieth anniversary in 2007, she issued a rare public statement, saying that she saw the struggle she and Richard waged as similar to the struggle of same-sex couples today:

> My generation was bitterly divided over something that should have been so clear and right. The majority believed...that it was God's plan to keep people apart, and that government should discriminate against people in love. But...[t]he older generation's fears and prejudices have given way, and today's young people realize that if someone loves someone they have a right to marry. Surrounded as I am now by wonderful children and grandchildren, not a day goes by that I don't think of Richard and our love, our right to marry, and how much it meant to me to have that freedom to marry the person precious to me, even if others thought he was the "wrong kind of person" for me to marry. I believe all Americans, no matter their race, no matter their sex, no matter their sexual orientation, should have that same freedom to marry.[13]

The politics of humanity may seem to require us to agree with her. Let us consider, however, the arguments on the other side.

3. THE PANIC OVER SAME-SEX MARRIAGE: ARGUMENTS,
CONTAMINATION FEARS

As we examine the arguments against same-sex marriage, we must
keep two questions firmly in mind. First, does each argument really
justify legal restriction of same-sex marriage, or only some people's
attitudes of moral and religious disapproval? We live in a country in
which people have a wide range of different religious beliefs, and
we agree in respecting the space within which people pursue those
beliefs. We do not, however, agree that these beliefs, by themselves,
are sufficient grounds for legal regulation. Typically, we understand
that some arguments (including some but not all moral arguments)
are public arguments bearing on the lives of all citizens in a decent
society, and others are intrareligious arguments. Thus, observant
Jews abhor the eating of pork, but few if any would think that this
religiously grounded abhorrence is a reason to make the eating of
pork illegal. The prohibition rests on religious texts that not all citizens embrace, and it cannot be translated into a public argument
that people of all religions can accept. Similarly in this case, we
must ask whether the arguments against same-sex marriage are
expressed in a neutral and sharable language, or only in a sectarian
doctrinal language. If the arguments are moral rather than doctrinal,
they fare better, but we still have to ask whether they are compatible with core values of a society dedicated to giving all citizens the
equal protection of the laws. Many legal aspects of our history of
racial and gender-based discrimination were defended by secular
moral arguments, but that did not insulate them from constitutional
scrutiny.

Second, we must ask whether each argument justifies its conclusion, or whether there is reason to see the argument as a rationaliza-
tion of some deeper sort of anxiety or aversion (animus, to use the
language of *Romer*).

The first and most widespread objection to same-sex marriage is that it is immoral and unnatural. Similar arguments were widespread in the antimiscegenation debate, and in both cases, these arguments are typically made in a sectarian and doctrinal way, referring to religious texts. (Antimiscegenation judges, for example, referred to the will of God in arguing that racial mixing is unnatural.) It is difficult to cast such arguments in a form that could be accepted by citizens whose religion teaches something different. They look like Jewish arguments against the eating of pork: good reasons for members of some religions not to engage in same-sex marriage, but not sufficient reasons for making them illegal in a pluralistic society.

A second objection, and perhaps the one that is most often heard from thoughtful people, insists that the main purpose of state-sanctified marriage is procreation and the rearing of children. Protecting an institution that serves these purposes is a legitimate public interest, and so there is a legitimate public interest in supporting potentially procreative marriages. Does this mean there is also a public interest in restricting marriage to only those cases where there may be procreation? This is less clear. We should all agree that the procreation, protection, and safe rearing of children are important public purposes. It is not clear, however, that we have ever thought these important purposes best served by restricting marriage to the potentially procreative. If we ever did think like this, we certainly haven't done anything about it. We have never limited marriage to the fertile, or even to those of an age to be fertile. It is very difficult, in terms of the state's interest in procreation, to explain why the marriage of two heterosexual seventy-year olds should be permitted and the marriage of two men or two women should be forbidden—all the more since so many same-sex couples have and raise children. If the proposal were to introduce new restrictions—marriage only for the potentially procreative—it might make sense, though we'd want to know why the restriction helps the procreators.

But it's clear few would support such a restriction. We are all more likely to agree with Milton: marriage is about more than the merely biological. It is about companionship, conversation, a shared life.

As it stands, then, the procreation argument looks two-faced, approving in heterosexuals what it refuses to tolerate in same-sex couples. If the arguer should add that sterile heterosexual marriages somehow support the efforts of the procreative, we can reply that gay and lesbian couples who don't have or raise children may support, similarly, the work of procreative couples.

Sometimes this argument is put a little differently: marriage is about the protection of children, and we know that children do best in a home with one father and one mother, so there is a legitimate public interest in supporting an institution that fulfills this purpose. Put this way, the argument, again, offers a legitimate public reason to favor and support heterosexual marriage, though it is less clear why it gives a reason to restrict same-sex marriage (and marriages of those too old to have children, or not desiring children). Its main problem, however, is with the facts. Again and again, psychological studies have shown that children do best when they have love and support, and it appears that two-parent households do better at that job than single-parent households. There is no evidence, however, that opposite-sex couples do better than same-sex couples. There is a widespread feeling that these results can't be right, that living in an immoral atmosphere must be bad for the child. But that feeling rests on the religious judgments of the first argument; when the well-being of children is assessed in a religiously neutral way, there is no difference.[14] Moreover, there is surely no evidence that the recognition of same-sex marriage would diminish the number of couples who choose traditional marriage and bring up children within that institution. So even if one had reason to think that setting best for children, the prohibition of same-sex marriage does nothing to promote child welfare, so construed.

A third argument is that by conferring state approval on something that many people believe to be evil, same-sex marriage will force them to "bless" or approve of it, thus violating their conscience. This argument was recently made in an influential way by Charles Fried in *Modern Liberty*. Fried, who, as we saw in chapter 2, supports an end to sodomy laws and expresses considerable sympathy with same-sex couples, still thinks that marriage goes too far because of this idea of enforced approval.

What, precisely, is the argument here? Fried does not suggest that the recognition of same-sex marriage would violate the Free Exercise Clause of the First Amendment—and that would be an implausible position to take. Presumably, then, the position is that the state has a legitimate interest in banning same-sex marriage on the grounds that it offends many religious believers.

This argument contains many difficulties. First, it raises an Establishment Clause problem: for, as we've seen, religions vary greatly in their attitude to same-sex marriage, and the state, following this argument, would be siding with one group of believers against another. More generally, there are a lot of things that a modern state does that people deeply dislike, often on religious grounds. Public education teaches things that many religious parents abhor (such as evolution and the equality of women); parents often choose homeschooling for that reason. Public health regulations license butchers who cut up pigs for human consumption; Jews who observe the dietary laws don't want to be associated with this practice. But nobody believes that Jews have a right to ask the state to impose their religiously grounded preference on all citizens. The Old Order Amish don't want their children to attend public school past age fourteen, holding that such schooling is destructive of community. The state respects that choice—for Amish children; and the state even allows Amish children to be exempt from some generally applicable laws for reasons of religion. But nobody would dream of thinking that the Amish have a right to expect the state to make public schooling past age fourteen off-limits for all children. Part of life in a pluralistic society that values the nonestablishment of religion is an attitude of live and let live. Whenever we see a nation that does allow the imposition of religiously grounded preferences on all citizens—as with some Israeli laws limiting activity on the Sabbath, and as with laws in India banning cow slaughter—we see a nation with a religious establishment, de jure or de facto. We have chosen not to take that route, and for good reasons. To the extent that we choose workdays, holidays, and so on that coincide with the preferences of a religious majority, we bend over backward to be sensitive to the difficulties this may create for minorities.

A fourth argument, again appealing to a legitimate public purpose, focuses on the difficulties that traditional marriage seems to be facing in our society. Pointing to rising divorce rates and evidence that children are being damaged by lack of parental support, people say that we need to defend traditional marriage, not to undermine it by opening the institution to those who don't have any concern for its traditional purposes. We could begin by contesting the characterization of same-sex couples. In large numbers, they do have and raise children. Marriage, for them as for others parents, provides a clear framework of entitlements and responsibilities, as well as security, legitimacy, and social standing for their children. In fact, the states that have legalized same-sex marriage, Massachusetts and Connecticut, have among the lowest divorce rates in the nation, and the Massachusetts evidence shows that the rate has not risen as a result of the legalization.

We might also pause before granting that an increase in the divorce rate signals social degeneration. In the past women often stayed married, enduring neglect and even abuse, because they had no marketable skills and no employment options. It is evident that one factor involved in modern divorce is the autonomy of women, and we should not lament the freedom of choice that increasing opportunities make available. We should also bear in mind the increased life span. By some calculations, marriages are not shorter today than they used to be, it's just that people live so much longer. Just as many people go through more than one career these days, so they may go through more than a single marriage. This may not always be bad. The human life span is shifting.

But let us concede, for the sake of argument, that there is a social problem. What, then, about the claim that legalizing same-sex marriage would undermine the effort to defend or protect traditional marriage? If society really wants to defend traditional marriage, as it surely is entitled to do and probably ought to do, many policies suggest themselves: family and medical leave; drug and alcohol counseling on demand; generous support, in health policies, for marital counseling and mental health treatment; stronger laws against domestic violence and better enforcement of these laws; employment counseling and financial support for those under stress during economic crises; and, of course, tighter enforcement of child support laws. Such measures have a clear relationship to the stresses and strains facing traditional marriage. The prohibition of same-sex marriage does not. If we were to study all recent cases of heterosexual divorce, we would be unlikely to find even a single case in which the parties (or an objective onlooker) felt that their divorce was caused by the availability of marriage to same-sex couples. Divorce is usually an intimate personal matter bearing on the nature of the marital relationship. And it isn't even expensive to legalize same-sex marriage, so such a change wouldn't compete for resources with the others I've mentioned.

The objector at this point typically makes a further move. The very recognition of same-sex marriage on a par with traditional marriage demeans traditional marriage, makes it less valuable. What's being said, it seems, is something like this: if the Metropolitan Opera auditions started giving prizes to pop singers of the sort who sing on the television show *American Idol*, this would contaminate the opera world. Similarly, including in the Hall of Fame baseball players who got their records by cheating on the drug rules would contaminate the Hall of Fame, cheapening the real achievements of others. In general, the promiscuous recognition of low-level or nonserious contenders for an honor sullies the honor. This, I believe, is the sort of argument people are making when they assert that recognition of same-sex marriage defiles or undermines traditional marriage, when they talk about a "defense of marriage," and so forth. During the debates over the Defense of Marriage Act, and during the recent campaign in favor of Proposition 8 in California, many remarks in this vein were made. How should we evaluate this argument?

First of all, we may challenge it on the facts. Same-sex couples are not like B-grade singers or cheating athletes—or at least no more so than heterosexual couples. They want to get married for reasons very similar to those of heterosexuals: to express love and commitment, to gain religious sanctification for their union, to obtain a package of civil benefits—and, often, to have or raise children. Traditional marriage has its share of creeps, and there are same-sex creeps as well. But the existence of creeps among the heterosexuals has never stopped the state from marrying heterosexuals. Nor do people talk or think that way. I've never heard anyone say that the state's willingness to marry Britney Spears or O. J. Simpson demeans or sullies his or her own marriage. But somehow, without even knowing anything about the character or intentions of the same-sex couple next door, they think their own marriages would be sullied by public recognition of that union.

If the proposal were to restrict marriage to worthy people who have passed a character test, it would at least be consistent, though few would support such an intrusive regime. What is clear is that those who make this argument don't fret about the way in which unworthy or immoral heterosexuals could sully the institution of marriage or lower its value. Given that they don't worry about this, and given that they don't want to allow marriage for gays and lesbians who have proven their good character, it is difficult to take this argument at face value. The idea that same-sex unions will sully traditional marriage therefore cannot be understood without moving to the terrain of disgust and contamination. The only distinction between unworthy heterosexuals and the class of gays and lesbians that can possibly explain the difference in people's reaction is that the sex acts of the former do not disgust the majority, whereas the sex acts of the latter do. The thought must be that to associate traditional marriage with the sex acts of same-sex couples is to defile or contaminate it, in much the way that eating food served by a *dalit* used to be taken by many people in India to contaminate the high-caste body. Nothing short of a primitive idea of stigma and taint can explain the widespread feeling that same-sex marriage defiles or contaminates straight marriage, while the marriages of immoral and sinful heterosexuals do not do so.

If the arguer should reply that marriage between two people of the same sex cannot result in the procreation of children, and so must be a kind of sham marriage, which insults or parodies and thus demeans the real sort of marriage—an argument often made[15]—we are right back to the second argument. And we have to say, first, that marriage has never required procreation—even in the history of the Roman Catholic Church, which has always been willing to marry sterile older couples. Those who insist so strongly on procreation do not feel sullied or demeaned or tainted by the presence next door of two opposite-sex seventy-year-olds newly married, nor by the presence of opposite-sex couples who publicly announce their intention never to have children. They do not try to get lawmakers to make such marriages illegal, and they neither say nor feel that such marriages are immoral or undermine their own. So the feeling of undermining or demeaning cannot honestly be explained by the point about children, and must be explained instead by other darker ideas.

If we're looking for a historical parallel to the anxieties associated with same-sex marriage, we can find it in the history of views about miscegenation. At the time of *Loving v. Virginia*, in 1967, sixteen states both prohibited and punished marriages across racial lines. In Virginia, a typical example, such a marriage was a felony punishable by from one to five years in prison. Like same-sex marriages, cross-racial unions were opposed with a variety of arguments, both political and theological. In hindsight, however, we can see that disgust was at work. Indeed, it did not hide its hand: the idea of racial purity was proudly proclaimed (e.g., in the Racial Integrity Act of 1924 in Virginia), and ideas of taint and contamination were ubiquitous. If people felt disgusted and contaminated by the thought that a black person had drunk from the same public drinking fountain, or gone swimming in the same public swimming pool, or used the same toilet, or the same plates and glasses—all widely held Southern views—we can see that the thought of sex and marriage between black and white would have carried a powerful freight of revulsion. The Supreme Court concluded that such ideas of racial stigma were the only ideas that really supported those laws, whatever else was said: "There is patently no legitimate overriding purpose independent of invidious racial discrimination which justifies this classification."[16]

We should draw the same conclusion about the prohibition of same-sex marriage: irrational ideas of stigma and contamination, the sort of "animus" the Court recognized in *Romer*, is a powerful force in its support. So thought the Supreme Court of Connecticut in October 2008, saying:

> Beyond moral disapprobation, gay persons also face virulent homophobia that rests on nothing more than feelings of revulsion

toward gay persons and the intimate sexual conduct with which they are associated.... Such visceral prejudice is reflected in the large number of hate crimes that are perpetrated against gay persons.... The irrational nature of the prejudice directed at gay persons, who "are ridiculed, ostracized, despised, demonized and condemned" merely for being who they are... is entirely different in kind than the prejudice suffered by other groups that previously have been denied suspect or quasi-suspect class status.... This fact provides further reason to doubt that such prejudice soon can be eliminated and underscores the reality that gay persons face unique challenges to their political and social integration.[17]

We have now seen the arguments against same-sex marriage. They do not seem particularly impressive. We have not seen any that would supply government with a compelling state interest, and it seems likely, given *Romer*, that these arguments, motivated by animus, fail even the rational basis test.

The argument in favor of same-sex marriage is straightforward: if two people want to make a commitment of the marital sort, they should be permitted to do so, and excluding one class of citizens from the benefits and dignity of that commitment demeans them and insults their dignity.

4. WHAT IS THE "RIGHT TO MARRY"?

In our constitutional tradition, there is frequent talk of a "right to marry."[18] In *Loving v. Virginia*, the case that invalidated the laws against miscegenation, the Court calls marriage "one of the basic civil rights of man." A later case, *Zablocki v. Redhail*, recognizes the right to marry as a fundamental right for Fourteenth Amendment purposes, apparently under the Equal Protection Clause; the Court states that "the right to marry is of fundamental importance for all individuals," and continues with the observation that "the decision to marry has been placed on the same level of importance as decisions relating to procreation, childbirth, child rearing, and family relationships."[19] Before courts can sort out the issue of same-sex marriage, they have to try to figure out two things: (1) what does this "right to marriage" mean? And (2) who has it?

What does the "right to marriage" mean? On a minimal understanding, it just means that if the state chooses to offer a particular package of expressive or civil benefits under the name "marriage," it must make that package available to all who seek that status without discrimination (though here "all" will require further interpretation). *Loving* concerned the exclusion of interracial couples from the institution; *Zablocki*, similarly, concerned the attempt of the state of Wisconsin to exclude from marriage parents who could not show that they had met their child support obligations. Another pertinent early case, *Skinner v. Oklahoma*, invalidated a law mandating the compulsory sterilization of the "habitual criminal," saying that such a person, being cut off from "marriage and procreation," would be "forever deprived of a basic liberty."[20] A more recent case, *Turner v. Safley*, invalidated a prohibition on marriages by prison inmates in the Missouri state prison system.[21] All the major cases, then, turn on the denial to a particular group of people of an institutional package already available to others.

Is the right to marry, then, merely a nondiscrimination right? If so, the state is not required to offer marriages at all. It's only that once it does so, it must do so with an even hand. The talk of marriage as a fundamental right, together with the fact that most of these decisions mingle equal protection analysis with due process considerations, suggests, however, that something further is being said. What is it? Would it violate the Constitution if a state decided that it would offer only civil unions and drop the status of marriage, leaving that for religious and private bodies?

Put in terms of our three categories, then, does the "right to marry" obligate a state to offer a set of economic and civil benefits to married people? Does it obligate a state to confer dignity and status on certain unions by the use of the term "marriage"? And does it require the state to recognize or validate unions approved by religious bodies? Clearly, the answer to the third question is, and has always been, "no." Many marriages that are approved by religious bodies are not approved by the state, as the case of same-sex marriage has long shown us, and nobody has thought it promising to contest these denials on constitutional grounds. The right to the free exercise of religion clearly does not require the state to approve whatever marriages a religious body approves.

It is also pretty clear that the "right to marry" does not obligate the state to offer any particular package of civil benefits to people who marry. This has repeatedly been said in cases dealing with the marriage right.

On the other side, however, it's pretty clear that the right in question is not simply a right to be treated like others, without group-based discrimination. The right to marry is frequently classified with fundamental personal liberties protected by the Due Process Clause of the Fourteenth Amendment. In *Meyer v. Nebraska*, for example, the Court says that the liberty protected by that clause "without doubt...denotes not merely freedom from bodily restraint but also the right of the individual to contract, to engage in any of the common occupations of life, to acquire useful knowledge, to marry, establish a home and bring up children, to worship God according to the dictates of his own conscience, and generally to enjoy those privileges long recognized...as essential to the orderly pursuit of happiness by free men."[22] *Loving* similarly states that "the freedom to marry, or not marry, a person of another race resides with the individual and cannot be infringed by the state," grounding this conclusion in the Due Process Clause as well as the Equal Protection Clause. *Zablocki* allows that "reasonable regulations that do not significantly interfere with decisions to enter into the marital relationship may legitimately be imposed," but concludes that the Wisconsin law goes too far, violating the rights guaranteed by the Due Process Clause. With related arguments, *Turner v. Safley* determines that the restriction of prisoner marriages violates the Due Process Clause's privacy right. Significantly, in that same case the Court upheld a very tough restriction on the First Amendment right of correspondence by prisoners, so it was clear that the status of marriage as a fundamental liberty was being affirmed.

What does due process liberty mean in this case? Most of the cases concern attempts by the state to forbid a class of marriages. That sort of state interference with marriage is, apparently, unconstitutional on due process as well as equal protection grounds. So, if a state forbade everyone to marry, that would presumably be unconstitutional.

It is plausible to suggest that the denial of divorce, or excessively burdensome restrictions on divorce, could also come under constitutional scrutiny under this construction, and the Court has moved cautiously in this direction. In *Boddie v. Connecticut*,[23] the Court held that the Due Process Clause prevents any state from denying divorce to indigents on the grounds that they cannot pay the filing fees. They supported their argument with reference to the "right to marry" cases and insisted that the "basic position" of marriage in our society, combined with the state's monopoly of divorce, entailed that this financial impediment to divorce is unconstitutional. In *Sosna v. Iowa*,[24] however, the Court upheld Iowa's residency requirement, challenged on both due process and equal protection grounds, as a reasonable exercise of state power.

Nowhere, however, has the Court held that a state must offer the expressive benefits of marriage. There would appear to be no constitutional barrier to the decision of a state to get out of the expressive game altogether, going over to a regime of civil unions, or, even more extremely, to a regime of private contract for marriages, in which the state plays the same role it plays in any other contractual process.

Again, the issue turns on equality. What the cases consistently hold is that when the state does offer a status that has both civil benefits and expressive dignity, it must offer it with an even hand. This position, which I've called "minimal," is not so minimal when one looks into it. Laws against miscegenation were in force in sixteen states at the time of *Loving*. The prison regulation in *Turner* seemed a very obvious part of the discretionary power of prison wardens.

In other words, marriage is a fundamental liberty right of individuals, and because it is that, it also involves an equality dimension: groups of people cannot be fenced out of that fundamental right without some overwhelming reason. It's like voting: there isn't a constitutional right to vote, as such—some jobs can be filled by appointment. But the minute voting is offered, because of its fundamental status it is unconstitutional to fence out a group of people from the exercise of the right. At this point, then, the question becomes: Who has this liberty/equality right to marry? And what reasons are strong enough to override it?

Who has the right? At one extreme, it seems clear that, under existing law, the state that offers marriage is not required to allow it to polygamous unions. Whatever one thinks about the moral issues involved in polygamy, our constitutional tradition has upheld a law making polygamy criminal, so it is clear, at present, that polygamous unions do not have equal recognition. (The legal arguments against polygamy, however, are extremely weak. The primary state interest that is strong enough to justify legal restriction is an interest in the equality of the sexes, which would not tell against a regime of sex-equal polygamy.)

Regulations on incestuous unions have also typically been thought to be reasonable exercises of state power, although, here again, the state interests have been defined very vaguely. The interest in preventing child abuse would justify a ban on most cases of parent-child incest, but it's unclear that there is any strong state interest that should block adult brothers and sisters from marrying. (The health risk involved is no greater than in many cases where marriage is permitted.) Nonetheless, it's clear that if a brother-sister couple challenged such a restriction today on due process/equal protection grounds, they would lose, because the state's alleged (health) interest in forbidding such unions would prevail. (States vary a good deal in their definition of incest, and first cousins who want to get married may choose to move to another state, just as same-sex couples now do—with the difference that their marriage in the new state will automatically be recognized in the old.[25])

How should we think of these cases? Should we think that these individuals have a right to marry as they choose, but that the state has a countervailing interest that prevails? Or should we think that they don't have the right at all, given the nature of their choices? I incline to the former view. On this view, the state has to show that the law forbidding such unions really is supported by a strong public interest.

At the other extreme, it is also clear that the liberty and equality rights involved in the right to marry do not belong only to the potentially procreative. *Turner v. Safley* concerned marriages between inmates, most serving long terms, and outsiders—marriages that could not be consummated. The case rested on the emotional support provided by marriage and its religious and spiritual significance. At one point the Court mentions, as an additional factor, that the inmate may someday be released, so that the marriage might be consummated, but that is clearly not the basis of the holding. Nor does any other case suggest that the elderly or the sterile do not have the right.

The best way of summarizing the tradition seems to be this: all adults have a right to choose whom to marry. They have this right because of the emotional and personal significance of marriage, as well as its procreative potential. This right is fundamental for due process purposes, and it also has an equality dimension. No group of people may be fenced out of this right without an exceedingly strong state justification. It would seem that the best way to think about the cases of incest and polygamy is that in these cases the state can meet its burden by showing that policy considerations outweigh the individual's right, although it is not impossible to imagine that these judgments might change over time. What, then, of people who seek to marry someone of the same sex?

5. MASSACHUSETTS, CONNECTICUT, CALIFORNIA, IOWA: LEGAL ISSUES

This is the question with which courts are currently wrestling. To date, courts in Massachusetts, California, Connecticut, and Iowa have ruled that marriage must be offered to same-sex couples, although the passage of Proposition 8 in California means that same-sex marriage is no longer legal there. Meanwhile, Maine and New Hampshire have legalized same-sex marriage by legislative action. (Earlier, Hawaii's Supreme Court ruled that same-sex couples must be permitted to marry, but a constitutional amendment overturned that ruling.) Both California and Connecticut already had enacted legislatively a regime of civil unions that gave all the privileges and benefits of marriage (at least for in-state purposes), so the expressive issue was front and center.

Although the legislation in Main and New Hampshire is of key significance, showing that democratic majorities can support same-sex marriage, let us focus from now on on the four court decisions, since our topic is constitutional law. All four courts had to answer four questions (using not only federal constitutional law, but also the text and tradition of their own state constitutions): First, will civil unions suffice, or is the status of marriage constitutionally compelled? Second, is this issue one of due process or equal protection, or a complex mixture of both? Third, in assessing the putative right against the countervailing claims of state interest, is sexual orientation a suspect classification for equal protection purposes? In other words, does the state forbidding such unions have to show a mere rational basis for the law, or a compelling state interest? Fourth, what interests might so qualify?

The four states give different answers to these questions, but there is a large measure of agreement. All agree that, as currently practiced, marriage is a status with a strong component of public dignity. Because of that unique status, it is fundamental to individual self-definition, autonomy, and the pursuit of happiness. The right to marry does not oblige states to offer any particular package of benefits, but it does oblige them to "protect the core elements of the family relationship from at least some types of improper interference by others."[26] The right does not belong only to the potentially procreative. (The Massachusetts court notes, for example, that people who cannot stir from their deathbeds are still permitted to marry.)

For all these expressive reasons, it seems that civil unions are a kind of second-class status, lacking the affirmation and recognition characteristic of marriage. It is the difference of status—especially when understood against the history of discrimination against gays and lesbians—that makes the separate-but-allegedly-equal regimes of California and Massachusetts constitutionally problematic. As the

California court put it, the right is not a right to a particular word; it is the right "to have their family relationship accorded dignity and respect equal to that accorded other officially recognized families." Massachusetts, California, and Connecticut draw on the miscegenation cases to make this point. (Iowa instead focuses on the history of Iowans' strong opposition to all forms of legal inequity.) The California court notes that if states formerly opposed to miscegenation had created a separate category called "transracial union," while still denying interracial couples the status of "marriage," we would easily see that it was no solution.

Three of the four courts invoke both due process and equal protection. (Iowa mentions liberty briefly, but the analysis dwells on equal protection alone.) The Massachusetts court notes that the two guarantees frequently "overlap, as they do here." They all agree that the right to marry is an individual liberty right that also involves an equality component: a group of people can't be fenced out of that right without a very strong governmental justification.

How strong? Here the states diverge. The Massachusetts court held that the denial of same-sex marriages fails to pass even the rational basis test. In reaching that conclusion, it considers a variety of arguments against same-sex marriage but concludes that they are so inconsistent with current practice (for example, the marriage-for-procreation argument flies in the face of the way marriage is in fact administered) or so nebulous (the argument that same-sex marriage will "trivialize or destroy" traditional marriage) that they do not meet even a minimal standard of review.

The California, Connecticut, and Iowa courts, by contrast, held that sexual orientation is a suspect classification. The Connecticut and Iowa courts, which have traditionally recognized three distinct levels of equal protection scrutiny, held that classifications involving sexual orientation, like classifications involving gender, require intermediate scrutiny (unlike classifications involving race, which get strict scrutiny). The California court, which has traditionally had only two levels of review, held that sexual orientation requires strict scrutiny, also analogizing sexual orientation to gender.

In the process, California and Connecticut argue explicitly against the thesis that sexual orientation discrimination is best understood as sex-based discrimination. Along with Iowa, they argue in favor of the thesis supported in chapter 4, that sexual orientation itself is a suspect classification.[27] The two discussions of the criteria for suspect classification are very thorough—indeed, they mark an advance on the Supreme Court's discussions of this question. They come to the same conclusion: the central criteria for suspect classification are a *history of discrimination* and the *lack of relevance* of the characteristic to the social functions in question. Political powerlessness is significant only against the background of the history of discrimination, and it basically means that the group has not yet progressed far enough for us to be confident that the democratic process will treat it fairly. Immutability is relevant only as a sign that the characteristic is not germane to many functions, and, as the Iowa court usefully adds, as a proxy for the thought that the characteristic is a deep part of people's identity and sense of self, so it is unreasonable to ask them to change it.

A striking section of the Connecticut opinion concerns the particularly vicious irrational form of the prejudice against gays and lesbians. Here the court recognizes the politics of disgust, in the passage I quoted at the end of section 3, concluding that this revulsion is so powerful that it gives reason to think that democratic processes cannot possibly treat the claims of same-sex couples in an evenhanded manner. Only racial and religious groups, they conclude, have ever suffered similarly violent hatred.

What state interests lie on the other side? The California, Connecticut, and Iowa opinions examine carefully the main contenders, concluding that none rises to the level of a compelling interest. Preserving tradition all by itself cannot be such an interest: as the Connecticut court writes, "the justification of 'tradition' does not explain the classification, it just repeats it." Nor can discrimination be justified simply on the grounds that legislators have strong convictions. None of the other proffered policy considerations (the familiar ones we have already identified) stands up as sufficiently strong.

These opinions will not convince everyone. Nor will all who like their conclusion, or even their reasoning, agree that it's good for courts to handle this issue, rather than democratic majorities. But the opinions, I believe, should convince a reasonable person that constitutional law, and therefore courts, have a legitimate role to play in this divisive area, at least sometimes. The reasoning of the opinions is respectful of opposing positions, detailed, and labored. (Indeed the extraordinary length of the opinions shows the justices bending over backward to address the opposition.) As legal reasoning it is extremely well done. In the process, the opinions, full of examples of prejudice, give good reason to think that democratic majorities can't yet be trusted to put aside bigotry in order to confront this issue in a fair-minded way. That is exactly the sort of situation in which judges have a legitimate role to play, standing up for minorities whose fundamental rights have not been given a fair hearing in the majoritarian political process.

A significant aspect of the Iowa opinion is its sensitivity to the challenge to courts' authority. The law that the court is declaring unconstitutional was passed rather recently, in 1998. So in that sense it has strong democratic credentials. Throughout the opinion, however, the court emphasizes more general aspects of Iowa's history that lead toward a concern for equality, even when the minority concerned is unpopular. The very first reported case of the Supreme Court of Iowa, they remind their readers, was one in which "we refused to treat a human being as property to enforce a contract for slavery"—seventeen years before the infamous *Dred Scott* decision, in which the U.S. Supreme Court upheld the right to treat a person as mere property. Iowa was also the first state in the union to admit a woman to the practice of law—in 1869, four years before the U.S. Supreme Court upheld an Illinois law denying women the right to practice law. "In each of those instances, our state approached a fork in the road toward fulfillment of our constitution's ideals and reaffirmed the 'absolute equality of all' persons before the law as 'the very foundation principle of our government.'" The current case is then compared to that illustrious sequence. What the court is suggesting is that Iowa's court decisions, though controversial (probably even in Iowa) at the time, now seem right, bold, and ahead of the nation. Their message clearly is: you see how these bold court decisions give you something to be proud of as Iowans. Let us once again keep Iowa in the vanguard of the nation's progress toward equality.

Same-sex marriage is a good issue for federalism to handle, at least for a while. While it raises fundamental issues of personal liberty and dignity, and thus is in principle suited for a sweeping Supreme Court judgment such as *Loving*, none can doubt that at the present time such a decision would politicize the Court and polarize public opinion. The existence of same-sex marriage, over time, is showing and will continue to show that the main objections are in error: nothing new and terrible will happen to heterosexuals, who will no doubt continue to face the same marital problems they had before. Children will continue to be at risk, but it will become clear that the risk comes from inadequate health care and economic support, not from the same-sex couple living next door. As some states experiment with same-sex marriage, some others try civil unions, and some others recognize same-sex marriages legally contracted elsewhere, people will learn more about the institution, and democratic preferences are highly likely to change. None of that would have started, however, had at least some state courts not had the daring to read their constitutions with a courageous and unbiased eye.

6. THE FUTURE OF MARRIAGE

What ought we to hope and work for, as a just future for families in our society? Should government continue to marry people at all? Should it drop the expressive dimension and simply offer civil union packages? Should it back away from package deals entirely, in favor of a regime of disaggregated benefits and private contract? Such questions, the penumbra of any constitutional debate, require us to identify the vital rights and interests that need state protection and to think how to protect them without impermissibly infringing either equality or individual liberty. Our analysis of the constitutional issues does not dictate specific answers to these questions, but it does constrain the options we ought to consider.

Many structures demand serious consideration, ranging from a more inclusive version of marriage as we now know it to a regime of private contract with governmental protections for children and elderly dependents. If constructed in such a way as to protect equal access and the due process liberty rights that we have identified, both of these solutions would seem to pass constitutional muster—although it would clearly be unconstitutional for a state to withdraw marriage and substitute civil unions for all in order to avoid recognizing same-sex marriage. (This would be analogous to the way in which, in the South, attempts were made to close public schools and swimming pools to avoid having to integrate them.) The choice between various options will flow from policy considerations rather than from constitutional law.

A key question must be whether government should continue to offer a package of benefits similar to those offered in today's institution of marriage, or whether those benefits ought to be disaggregated and attached to a variety of distinct relationships. (People who share a household may not be sexual partners, and committed sexual partners may have separate finances.) Our analysis suggests that constitutional law does not require the state to offer any particular package of benefits. The disaggregated approach would pass constitutional muster if both equal access and due process liberty were sufficiently protected. I believe that there are many reasons to favor such disaggregated rethinking, both about the interests that need protection and about the different groups that might receive entitlements. The arguments for this conclusion, however, would carry us well beyond our present topic.

And what about the name "marriage"? It is so divisive today, and it is also so capricious in its meaning. (If it means dignity, why do we give it so easily to heterosexuals? If it doesn't mean dignity, why are people so upset about the idea that it might be given to same-sex couples?) Might a good solution be for the state to back out of the expressive domain altogether, offering civil unions for both same-sex and opposite-sex couples? Our analysis suggests that the Constitution does not require the state to use this particular name rather than some other, although it does require the state to protect people's (equal) liberty in setting up households. I personally favor the solution of leaving civil unions to the state and marriage to religions and other private entities, but arguing for this position would carry me well beyond our legal topic. Certainly states may not stop marrying couples just in order to avoid marrying same-sex couples.

These important policy questions lie beyond the boundaries of the present book. To address them well, however, we need to understand the constraints the Constitution imposes, and it does impose strong constraints that have not yet been sufficiently acknowledged. We also need the same type of fearless scrutiny of history, values, and purposes that we find in the best examples of constitutional thought in this area.

The future of marriage looks, in one way, a lot like its past. People will continue to unite, form families, have children, and, sometimes, split up. What the Constitution dictates, however, is that whatever the state decides to do in this area will be done on a basis of equality. Government cannot exclude any group of citizens from the civil benefits or the expressive dignities of marriage without a compelling public interest. The full inclusion of same-sex couples is in one sense a large change, just as official recognition of interracial marriage was a large change, and just as the full inclusions of women and African-Americans as voters and citizens were large changes. On the other hand, those changes are best seen as a true realization of the promise contained in our constitutional guarantees. We should view this change in the same way. The politics of humanity asks us to stop viewing same-sex marriage as a source of taint or defilement to traditional marriage, but, instead, to understand the human purposes of those who seek marriage and the similarity of what they seek to that which straight people seek. When we think this way, the issue ought to look like the miscegenation issue: as an exclusion we can no longer tolerate, in a society pursuing equal respect and justice for all.

NOTES

1. Mill is speaking here of making marriage equal between the sexes, but the point applies, I believe, to the case at hand.

2. As we'll see in section 5, this has been explicitly established for prison inmates and noncustodial parents who fail to pay child support, perhaps the most extreme cases, in that states actually sought to deny marriage to these classes of people.

3. See Susan Treggiari, *Roman Marriage* (Oxford: Oxford University Press, 1991). Her study of grave inscriptions (*inter alia*) gives rich evidence

of what people sought in marriage and thought good to say about their marriages.

4. See the excellent treatment of marital norms in Craig Williams, *Roman Homosexuality* (New York: Oxford University Press, 1999).

5. Cicero, *Letters to Atticus* V.1 (number 94 in Shackleton Bailey's numbering), May 5 or 6, 51 BCE. I base my version on the wonderful translation of D. R. Shackleton Bailey for the Loeb Classical Library, though with some alterations. The word I translate "sympathy" is *humanitas*, for Cicero a key virtue involving empathetic understanding and delicacy of manner.

6. In this section, I draw primarily on Nancy F. Cott, *Public Vows: A History of Marriage and the Nation* (Cambridge, MA: Harvard University Press, 2000), and Hendrik Hartog, *Man and Wife in America: A History* (Cambridge, MA: Harvard University Press, 2000).

7. Hartog, *Man and Wife in America*, 19.

8. See ibid., 18–19.

9. Ibid., 14.

10. Ibid.

11. See Andrew Koppelman, *Same Sex, Different States: When Same-Sex Marriages Cross State Lines* (New Haven, CT: Yale University Press, 2006).

12. See "Mildred Loving of *Loving v. Virginia* Speaks out about Marriage Equality," http://lesbianlife.about.com/od/gaymarriageinformation/a/Loving.htm.

13. Ibid.

14. On both of these questions, see the wide range of expert testimony summarized in Baehr v. Miike, Civ. No. 91–1394 (Hawaii Cir. Ct. Dec. 3, 1996). Remarkably, even the state's own experts for the most part agreed that sexual orientation is not an important indication of parental fitness.

15. For example, the *New York Times* of October 14, 2008, the day I first drafted this paragraph, carried a letter from a Roman Catholic priest to this effect.

16. *Loving v. Virginia*, 388 U.S. 1 (1967).

17. *Kerrigan v. Commissioner of Public Health.*

18. Throughout this section I have learned a lot from the excellent examination of this question in Cass R. Sunstein, "The Right to Marry," *Cardozo Law Review* 26 (2005): 2081–2120; though I differ with its analysis in several ways, it lays out the issue with incisiveness and clarity.

19. *Zablocki v. Redhail*, 434 U.S. 374, 384 (1978).

20. *Skinner v. Oklahoma*, 316 U.S. 535 (1942).

21. *Turner v. Safley*, 482 U.S. 78 (1987).

22. *Meyer v. Nebraska* 262, U.S. 390 (1923).

23. 401 U.S. 371 (1971).

24. 419 U.S. 393 (1975).

25. Even in the extreme case of uncle/niece marriage, allowed for Jews in Rhode Island on religious grounds, the binding nature of the marriage outside that state has been established.

26. As the California opinion states. Massachusetts: *Goodridge v. Department of Public Health*, 798 N.E. 2d 941 (Mass. 2003). California: *In re Marriage Cases* (2008) 43 Cal.4th 757 [76 Cal. Rptr. 3d 683, 183P. 3d 384]. Iowa: *Varnum v. Brien*, 763 N.W. 2d 862 (Iowa 2009).

27. The Koppelman thesis got one vote in Massachusetts.

CHAPTER SIX

Protecting Intimacy: Sex Clubs, Public Sex, Risky Choices

[T]he operation of live sex businesses contributes to the spread of sexually transmitted diseases and is "inimical to the health, safety, general welfare and morals of the inhabitants of the city of Phoenix" and...a "public nuisance per se."...The [police] memorandum also expressed concerns with cleanliness, nothing that the "potential exist [*sic*] for unwanted contact with different bodily fluids which include saliva, semen, blood, and fecal matter."

—*MUTSCHLER V. PHOENIX*,
ARIZONA COURT OF APPEALS, 2006

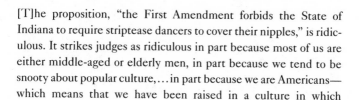

[T]he proposition, "the First Amendment forbids the State of Indiana to require striptease dancers to cover their nipples," is ridiculous. It strikes judges as ridiculous in part because most of us are either middle-aged or elderly men, in part because we tend to be snooty about popular culture,...in part because we are Americans—which means that we have been raised in a culture in which

Puritanism, philistinism, and promiscuity are complexly and often incongruously interwoven.

—JUDGE RICHARD POSNER,
CONCURRING OPINION IN *MILLER ET AL. V. CIVIL CITY OF SOUTH BEND*, 1990

I. DISGUST: ALIVE AND WELL

Sex is always a focus of social anxiety, but sex in group settings has been particularly scary to people in many times and places, raising fears of contagion and defilement that are grounded in the politics of disgust more than in any reason-based assessment of harms. Shakespeare's *Measure for Measure*, written during the spread of plague in London, which eventually closed the theaters in 1603, subtly links the sex trade with the plague and the closing of sex businesses with the (re)establishment of public health. So successful is the fictional regime depicted in that play in linking sex with images of disease that even Claudio, who had nonmarital intercourse with a woman whom he loves and to whom he was informally betrothed, thinks of their sexual acts as both dangerous and disgusting. He describes people's sexual desires, including his own, as "rats that ravin down their proper bane, a thirsty evil; and when we drink, we die." The procurer Lucio, by contrast, uses positive metaphors for sexuality, images of fertility and growth: but he is due to be suppressed, losing his livelihood, his positive attitude to sexuality being part of the disease the regime is determined to combat.

Today, similarly, we fear a plague—HIV/AIDS, and to a lesser degree other sexually transmitted diseases. Once again, live sex businesses are the targets of public anxiety. The idea of a "public health nuisance" has been prominently used to justify closing down live sex businesses ranging from adult bookstores to swinger clubs and gay bathhouses, and to impose restrictions on yet others (requiring, for example, that the dancers in striptease clubs cover their nipples and pubic area, or imposing burdensome licensing regulations and background checks on all employees).

When Paul Cameron used rhetoric relating gay sex to health risks, we could see that what was really going on was an appeal to disgust and primitive anxiety about bodily fluids. But we saw, too, that his extreme tactics no longer have much influence on the discussion of consensual conduct in the home. There, the politics of disgust is on the way out. In the same-sex marriage debate, the politics of disgust lurks beneath the surface, but it is well concealed by other, albeit inadequate, arguments. This chapter will show that, by contrast, the politics of disgust is alive and well, and out in the open, in America's legal and political dealings with sex businesses, bathhouses, and the like: non-homelike places where consenting adults meet to engage in sexual activity or watch erotic performances.

A variety of legal issues are involved here: the definition of *public nuisance* (which has a constitutional aspect, since it is relevant to the question of whether owners of sex businesses must be compensated for a "taking" when they are closed); the scope of the First Amendment freedom of expression; the proper understanding of the privacy right protected in *Lawrence*; and, more generally, the law's limits in policing consensual adult behavior. These issues do not all involve constitutional law, but they are interwoven in such a way that the constitutional issues cannot be well treated without an overview of the entire area.

Such questions do not concern same-sex actors only, and we shall examine cases dealing with primarily heterosexual swinger, S and M, and striptease clubs. Same-sex actors, however, face a heightened level of surveillance and disgust-anxiety, as the intense focus on gay bathhouses reveals. Because gay male behavior in particular has been hypersexualized in the public imaginary—depicted as a lifestyle emphasizing sexual promiscuity—it is easy to connect gay men to disease and defilement by focusing on venues (bathhouses, adult bookstores, restrooms) where casual sexual interactions take place, and then to stigmatize the entire community by associating it with a scare-image of these places as sites of disease. The stigmatization of swinger clubs and the like, by contrast, is not connected to widespread discrimination against the entire group of heterosexuals. Although all adults encounter a liberty deficit in this area, for gay men, it is also an issue of discrimination. It's not implausible for gay men to think that they cannot enjoy full social equality so long as panic-driven crusades against bathhouses and male sex clubs are a major part of social policy.

At the same time, because of the history of stigma, sex clubs and adult businesses have assumed considerable importance for both gays and lesbians as sites of protected social activity. Because until very recently gays who openly looked for sex and expressed desire in the wide range of places where heterosexuals may openly do so would be persecuted or even arrested, gay bars and other gay-friendly businesses became pivotal in the social self-definition of both gays and lesbians, and in the evolution of the gay rights movement itself. Because of this history, attacks on sex clubs and adult businesses have a centrality for gays and lesbians that they do not have for straights.

In this area we see the politics of disgust operating in a particularly ugly form, impinging on freedoms of association and expression and the equality of citizens. Devlin's politics of disgust plays a large role, and Mill's harm-based politics a small and inconsistent role. Often, too, apparently Millian arguments are so flimsy that they are mere masks for arguments based on disgust. The introduction of the appeal to disgust operates to short-circuit the search for reasons that will withstand rational scrutiny. We'll study the way in which the politics of disgust has confused the legal workings of the concept of "nuisance," and ask how, if at all, the principles in constitutional law that we have uncovered could help us think further about these problems. In the process, we'll see how our legal system's pervasive confusion over the concepts of "private" and "public" does yet further damage.

2. CLARIFYING CONCEPTS: HARM, NUISANCE, PRIVACY

When we examined Mill's distinction between self-regarding and other-regarding conduct, we considered three distinct types of activity. The first type causes, or imminently threatens to cause, harm to another; this sort of conduct is an uncontroversial candidate for legal regulation.[1] The second type produces what we called a *direct offense* that is harmlike in character: something offensive impinges on the activities of nonconsenting people in a way that jeopardizes their enjoyment of life. The third type has no direct impact on the lives of nonconsenting people (it is self-regarding in Mill's sense), though people may feel upset or disgusted when they merely imagine it going on. According to Mill, this is not a proper object of legal regulation. Our analysis of sodomy laws backs him up. Although our constitutional tradition has never accepted Mill's principle in full, it does accept something like it in certain privileged areas of intimate association.

The second type is the tricky one, and we now need to consider it further, because the boundary between the second and the third type is frequently blurred in legal discussions of sex clubs and "public" sex. Actions that are properly classified in our third category are often represented as if they belong in the second (potentially regulable) category, by an equivocation on the legal notion of nuisance. Let us turn, then, to the traditional law of nuisance.

Nuisance law protects people from something offensive or dangerous that interferes with their enjoyment of their activities or their property. The maxim often quoted is, *sic utere tuo ut alienum non laedas*, "use your own in such a way that you do no harm to that which is another's." In other words, a nuisance is a type of harm. Though the nuisance may be disgusting rather than violent, it does something that harms the recipient. That, in a nutshell, is our second category.

The classic precedent, quoted in virtually all modern nuisance cases, is Aldred's Case, which holds that a man has "no right to maintain a structure upon his own land, which, by reason of disgusting smells, loud or unusual noises, thick smoke, noxious vapors, the jarring of machinery, or the unwarrantable collection of flies, renders the occupancy of adjoining property dangerous, intolerable, or even uncomfortable to its tenants." The enumerated instances all involve something from person A's property coming onto the property of person B: either a discernible substance (flies, smoke, vapors), or sound waves and smells that are not just imaginary or conceptual, but real presences with a causal influence on B.[2] In other words, we are not dealing with our third category, where B is upset and disgusted merely because A is doing something on A's own property that B disliked. For a nuisance to be present, three conditions must typically be satisfied: (a) *causation*: B has caused something bad to happen to A, or to A's property; (b) *imposition*: B does not consent—the nuisance is an unwilling infliction; (c) *primary objects*: insofar as disgust is involved, the nuisance involves disgust at primary objects (bad odors, etc.)—frequently combined with real danger ("noxious vapors").

Cases in the modern tradition follow this lead. Many cases involve water rights: neighbor A may not contaminate water that flows through B's land. The case law makes it clear that strong sensory disgustingness is enough to constitute a nuisance.[3] Thus, the odors produced by a swine farm located in a residential area created a nuisance even though the odors were not injurious to health.[4] Similarly, a sewage lagoon near a dairy farm was held to be a nuisance even though it could not be demonstrated that its effluences actually harmed the cattle.[5] In these cases it is very important to note that our three essential conditions are satisfied: the nuisance is a physical substance that affects the recipient; the victim does not consent; and the disgust in question is disgust at primary objects, not a merely projective disgust (in which, for example, a certain class of persons or activities is found filthy or contaminating). A common citation, including all three of these conditions, is an 1875 text on nuisances by Horace Gay Wood:[6]

> But in reference to [water rights], as with the air, it is not every interference with the water that imparts impurities thereto, that is actionable, but only such as impart to the water such impurities as substantially impair its value for the ordinary purposes of life, and render it measurably unfit for domestic purposes; or such as causes unwholesome or offensive vapors or odors to arise from the water, and thus impairs the comfortable or beneficial enjoyment of property in its vicinity, or such as, while producing no actual sensible effect upon the water, are yet of a character calculated to disgust the senses, such as the deposit of the carcasses of dead animals therein, or the erection of privies over a stream, or any other use calculated to produce nausea or disgust in those using the water for the ordinary purposes of life, or such as impair its value for manufacturing purposes.[7]

That's the standard account of private nuisance. The law also recognizes a category of public nuisance, which is, basically, the extension of the account of private nuisance to cases where the impact is on the public at large.[8]

In chapter 3 we granted that public defecation and urination could be a nuisance to bystanders, and we could extend this to public sexual activity in which defecation and urination are involved. Other sexual activity is more difficult to fit into the nuisance category, but we granted that public masturbation and public sex might be squeezed in. Sexual secretions are among the primary objects of disgust; in many cases these sights and smells are unwillingly imposed on bystanders, and they represent a real physical presence impinging on the world of the bystander, not a merely constructive injury. In addition, many people believe that witnessing such activities causes harm to young people. So there are good reasons of Mill's sort to make these activities illegal.

Let's look more closely, however, at what we meant by "public" in that earlier discussion. What is problematic about public sex acts is that they take place in the presence of people who have not consented to witness them. There lies their link to the traditional category of nuisance: there is an intrusion. Let us imagine the sex acts taking place, instead, in a members-only club. Many such clubs, for unrelated reasons of corporate organization, are designated as "public accommodations." Here, however, the term "public" means something different: it would not suffice to make the sex acts nuisances in the classic sense—for direct imposition on unwilling viewers is absent. Because this is absent, our third element is also absent: disgust cannot be at primary objects when nonconsenting parties do not directly experience what is going on.

This case, then, belongs in our third category, not in our second. What upsets people is not what they see, hear, or smell: it is what they imagine to be taking place in those sex clubs. The ambiguity of the terms "public" and "private" confuses thought. In one sense the acts are public: they are in a facility that, for certain legal purposes, counts as a public accommodation. And they are not "private" if "private" means "in the home." But we argued that the contrast relevant to law is that between (relative) seclusion, meaning that no unwilling bystanders are affected, and being in a mixed surrounding composed of both consenting and nonconsenting parties. Let's keep that contrast in mind as we consider the use of nuisance law to police sex businesses.

3. SEX AND NUISANCE LAW

Most cities in the United States have laws against maintaining an establishment that is a "public health nuisance." Such establishments are subject to being closed down by public authorities. Moreover, if the establishment is a "public nuisance per se" (meaning "an act, occupation, or structure which is a nuisance at all times and under any circumstances, regardless of location or surroundings"[9]), owners need not be compensated for the property loss involved, because the closure does not count as a "taking." Examples include: "keeping diseased animals or the maintenance of a pond breeding malarial mosquitoes," a landfilling operation that would have the effect of flooding others' land, a nuclear power plant built over an earthquake fault.[10] Such examples are all nuisances in the classic Millian sense.

Sex businesses, in many city ordinances, are similarly classified as public nuisances. Consider these typical cases from Phoenix and New York:

> The operation of a business for purposes of providing the opportunity to engage in, or the opportunity to view, live sex acts is declared to be a disorderly house and a public nuisance per se which should be prohibited.
>
> (Phoenix City Code 223–54[A] [1] [1998])

> Prohibited Facilities: No establishment shall make facilities available for the purpose of sexual activities in which facilities

high risk sexual activity takes place. Such facilities shall constitute a public nuisance dangerous to the public health. "Establishment" shall mean any place in which entry, membership,
goods or services are purchased, "High Risk Sexual activity"
shall mean anal intercourse and fellatio.

(New York statute at issue in *City of New York
v. New Saint Mark's Baths*, 497)

What is the theory of nuisance used here? *Mutschler*, a case
involving the closing of a sex club under a Phoenix ordinance,
explaining the background of the law, states:

[T]he operation of live sex businesses contributes to the spread
of sexually transmitted diseases and is "inimical to the health,
safety, general welfare and morals of the inhabitants of the city
of Phoenix" and classifies the operation of a live sex acts business as a "public nuisance per se." ... The [police] memorandum
also expressed concerns with cleanliness, noting that the "potential exist [*sic*] for unwanted contact with different bodily fluids
which include saliva, semen, blood, and fecal matter."

Mutschler purports to give a Millian reason for the ordinance: sex
businesses cause health hazards for the general public. When we
inspect the reasoning further, however, disgust rears its head. Not,
however, disgust of the sort pertinent to the classic private nuisance
cases or their public analogues. No unwilling bystanders entered
Mutschler's club. The police claim to have been physically
disgusted, but they were there of their own volition. All the other
patrons were there because they wanted to participate in the swinger
activities for which the club was known. They paid an entrance fee,
and nobody was in any doubt about the nature of the club, which
was explicitly licensed as an adult business.

In what sense, then, could this business be described as a nuisance? (It's plain that the claim is that it is nuisance in the Millian sense, a danger to public health.) If the claim is that patrons of the club might contract venereal diseases, well, yes they might; but so might any person engaging in promiscuous sexual activity, and the patrons of a swinger club are people who are more likely than others to know the risks that their voluntary transactions involve. STDs are not contagious through the air or through casual contact; they are transmitted through sexual activity, and there is no allegation that any patrons are subjected to rape or other unwanted sexual conduct. Patrons of such a club are bound to be aware that some members have STDs, but it is their choice how they want to proceed in view of that risk. Of course an individual patron may always lie about his or her STD status, but the right response to that criminal act is to punish the deceiver, not to close the premises. The argument that the club is a nuisance to its own patrons is unconvincing.

Even weaker is a similar argument used, in connection with the spread of HIV/AIDS, to declare gay bathhouses a public nuisance. The relevant New York law unambiguously defines *public nuisance* in a Millian way: "whatever is dangerous to human life or detrimental to health." But where is the unwilling imposition? The gay community is aware of the virus, the risks it poses, and the mechanism of its transmission. (The community has also happily accepted, and in many cases voluntarily undertaken, measures warning patrons of the dangers of condomless sex and making condoms easily available.) HIV/AIDS can be transmitted only by the exchange of bodily fluids. So the most that can be said is that the bathhouses make it possible for men to engage in risky activities if they choose to do so.

But people choose to put themselves at risk in all sorts of ways in all sorts of activities. They climb mountains; they race cars; they box; they smoke; they overeat. Nobody suggests outlawing all of these activities. Some risky activities are regulated for safety: boxing has rules, and some municipalities now require fast-food restaurants to stop using trans-fats and to list the nutritional content of their offerings. Smoking is far more tightly regulated, but this is on account of the imposition of secondhand smoke on unwilling bystanders. Alcohol, a dangerous drug with well-documented links to harm to others (violence, drunk driving, sexual assault) is hardly regulated at all, except for age and place of purchase restrictions. In short, one cannot think of a nonsex case—apart from drug use, too complex to discuss here—in which an establishment promoting a purely self-regarding risky activity is closed down as a public nuisance. In all other cases, narrower options are pursued: to regulate, to educate, and to hold criminally liable anyone who by fraud lures a nonconsenting party into risks he or she has not agreed to run. Sexual activity, particularly same-sex activity, is unique in the degree of scrutiny it evokes.

Here again we see the politics of disgust in operation. Imagine the police report cited in *Mutschler* being rewritten as the study of a NASCAR rally. The same officers who express revulsion with risky behavior in the sex club would very likely extol the manliness on exhibit in the risky choice to drive unsafely. And yet the actual risk of serious bodily harm is likely to be far higher at NASCAR: there is no analogue to the condom for race car drivers. Neither, of course, poses a serious risk of harm for the nonparticipant.

One can find no more vivid example of the disgust-panic surrounding the culture of sex clubs in America than a controversy that broke out when my own university press wanted to publish *Unlimited Intimacy: Reflections on the Subculture of Barebacking*, by sex theorist Tim Dean, directory of the Humanities Institute and professor of English at the State University of New York at Buffalo. Dean's book is the first close anthropological study of the subculture of condomless sex in male sex clubs. Dean admits to being a member of that subculture; indeed, he could have gotten the information recorded in the book in no other way. The book studies the fantasies and wishes that propel this community, the self-conceptions of the people involved, the ideas that support the choice to engage in risky behavior. It focuses on consensual behavior with full disclosure of HIV status and is severely critical of deception. Essentially, it concludes that people who risk HIV infection by having sex without condoms are not pathological weirdos, but men driven by common male fantasies ("I'm a tough guy"; "I can take anything") and common calculations of cost and benefit (the extra pleasure of sex without a condom being thought more important than the risk, especially in a culture where disclosure is ethically mandated), and some of which are more surprising (fantasies of pregnancy and "breeding" in connection with viral transmission).

When the University of Chicago Press considered this volume—which had gone through the usual process of peer review and had been enthusiastically recommended by both referees and the editor in charge of this area—an intense controversy ensued. Many people were unwilling to see the press publish a book that could be seen as advocating "risky behavior." Never mind that Dean advocates nothing; his aim is to describe and to understand. The absence of stern moral condemnation seemed advocacy enough. The press would not have batted an eye had the editor recommended a book on mountain climbing or car racing or boxing or smoking or drinking; books on these topics are ubiquitously published by reputable publishers, including university presses. In the case of smoking, it's even possible to publish a book that extols the pleasures of smoking and denigrates the recent era of restriction. Sex, and particularly gay sex, was singled out for special scrutiny, as if frank talk about it was a kind of nuisance. Finally good sense and academic freedom prevailed, and the press decided to publish Dean's book; the anxiety it inspired, however, told an all-too-common story.

The idea that sex clubs are a nuisance because of the risks they pose for their own patrons cannot be coherently defended, particularly because lying about one's HIV status is already a criminal act. How could the club be said to be a nuisance to the general public? Shakespeare's *Measure for Measure*, written during an outbreak of plague, suggests, at least, that brothels are a place where diseases spread unwittingly from person to person: a person comes in for sex but also catches the plague—and then he goes out and spreads it to the nonconsenting general public.[11] Here there is at least a story to tell about how disease spreads to nonconsenting parties, though it is unclear why sex businesses would be singled out, when any crowded facility could serve the same purpose. Many of the play's characters already think of sex as inherently diseased or verminous (remember Claudio's reference to rats), so it would be all too easy to think of other diseases, too, as congregating in that place. In reality, however, the theater, the marketplace, a crowded restaurant—all these pose at least as great a risk of plague transmission. (London theaters were indeed closed in 1603 due to the outbreak.)

Plague, however, is contagious. Bubonic plague is transmitted by fleas, which can go from one person to another. Pneumonic plague, the sort that probably affected London in Shakespeare's time, is passed through sputum. Both can easily be spread in a confined and crowded setting to unwilling participants. HIV/AIDS does not work this way. It can be spread only by sexual contact, blood transfusions, organ donations, shared needles, and the like: in other words, by bodily fluids passing directly from one person to another. The virus dies very quickly in the air. So the case for calling the bathhouses, or any other sex business, a nuisance on the grounds that it is a risk to the general public is weak indeed.

If what is meant is that people will contract HIV in a sex club and then spread it to unwitting partners on the outside (spouses, new contacts), well, once again, we have provisions in the criminal law to deal with nondisclosure. If we consider, moreover, the place where such unwilling imposition most often takes place, namely in the marital bedroom, where husbands refuse to have sex with condoms and therefore force their wives to risk contracting a virus that the husband, straight or gay, has caught on the outside—the single greatest cause of the spread of HIV in Africa—we see that the remedy is not closing bathhouses or houses of prostitution, but reforming the marital consent norms and the willingness of police to intervene in cases of coercive sex within marriage, combined with solidarity among women against being forced to bear such risks. The protected zone of the home is currently one of the riskiest places to have sex.

Some of the cases invoke the notion of a "moral nuisance." What, precisely, is that? Three things seem to be meant. First is the pure Devlin claim: this is behavior that disgusts us when we imagine it going on. I've argued against this non-Millian reasoning throughout this book. In this area, though, the Devlin argument is often mixed up with alleged Millian reasons. The second thing people use the term *moral nuisance* to mean, then, is that the presence of a sex business in an area makes people in that area want to patronize the business; its presence therefore spreads a type of voluntary behavior that many people don't like. Usually such claims are not empirically supported, but suppose it's true that swinger clubs make more swingers in a given area: is that a reason to consider them a nuisance in the Millian sense? The elements of direct causation and unwilling imposition are lacking: they become swingers out of emulation, or convenience, or attraction, not through force.

The third meaning of moral nuisance, again allegedly Millian, is that sex businesses are magnets for various forms of unsavory or illegal activity. Often, as we'll see in the next section, empirical support for such claims is lacking or weak. But even were it strong, we need to distinguish two different types of secondary activities, if we care about Mill's categories. One type involves other self-regarding activities, such as prostitution. These activities may be illegal, but they involve only consenting parties, and they therefore don't constitute a nuisance in the Millian sense. They don't do anything directly to those who don't consent. Probably they should not be illegal at all, but that's another story.

The second type are truly harmful activities, such as rape and sexual assault, physical assault, deceptive drugging (e.g., of women with the "date rape drug"), and trafficking (prostitution involving force or fraud). It's not clear that bathhouses and swinger clubs are magnets for rapists. The average college fraternity probably generates more unwilling impositions on women than any such club. When people go to sex clubs, they are likely to be savvy and self-protective (unlike young women who go to frat parties).[12] Women who meet men over the internet and go to a secluded place to meet them are doing something far more unsafe than had they met the man in the confines of a sex club. If there is unwilling imposition in such a club, however, it should be handled directly by the criminal law, as it would be handled anywhere else. We should target criminals, not places of consensual activity that are sometimes patronized by criminals. (Nobody proposed closing restaurants known to be favorites of organized crime leaders.)

4. CONSTITUTIONAL PRINCIPLES? EQUAL PROTECTION, DUE PROCESS, FREEDOM OF EXPRESSION

Public nuisance laws are phobic and irrational. Are they, however, unconstitutional? Let's see whether the principles we have studied in previous chapters help us in this controversial area.

There has not yet been an Equal Protection Clause test of laws closing sex clubs, but we can imagine a scenario in which such a case would stand a good chance of success. Suppose a zoning law or some other type of public nuisance law singled out same-sex establishments for special restrictions. Or suppose that the ordinance itself was neutrally worded, but enforcement targeted same-sex establishments. In such a case, the law might well not survive rational basis review. Like the zoning law struck down in *Cleburne*, or the government program invalidated in *Moreno*, such an ordinance would appear to be motivated by mere animus. Since, however, Americans are phobic about public sex in general, not only when same-sex actors are involved, such a case may not materialize in the near future.

Lawrence, however, has already been used to defend some aspects of "public" sex. In conflicting opinions, two circuits of the Federal Court of Appeals upheld and struck down local ordinances banning the sale of sex toys.[13] Although the conflict will not soon be addressed by the Supreme Court, since Texas decided not to appeal in defense of its ban, the fascinating arguments show us how *Lawrence* is being read, and how it might gradually be extended to protect at least some aspects of sex in public accommodations.

In 1979, Texas rewrote its obscenity law to add a prohibition on the "promotion" (including "selling, giving, lending, distributing, or advertising") of "obscene devices," defined as any device "designed or marketed as useful primarily for the stimulation of human genital organs." In 1985, the Texas Court of Criminal Appeals held that the statute did not violate the constitutional right to privacy, since there was (in their view) no constitutional right to "stimulate... another's genitals with an object designed or marketed as useful primarily for that purpose."

Unlike the law at issue in *Griswold*, which criminalized both the provision and the use of contraceptive devices, the Texas law never criminalized use (although it did stipulate that the possession of six or more "obscene devices" would count as intent to "promote").

The statutes also added an affirmative defense for those who "promote" the devices for a bona fide "medical, psychiatric, judicial, legislative, or law enforcement purpose." (The Fifth Circuit noted that only three other states had similar laws in 2008: Mississippi, Alabama, and Virginia.) Given *Lawrence*, a group of retail sex toy merchants decided to mount a new challenge to the law.

Let's pause to ask what the legislators in these states are thinking. They cannot really believe that vibrators and dildos threaten public health. (Indeed, the plaintiffs in *Reliable Consultants* note that the use of sexual devices is often a way of limiting the spread of sexually transmitted diseases.) Anyone who looks seriously at risks to public health ought to acknowledge that, as sources of pleasure, sex toys threaten health far less than the sale of soft drinks and candy. So, opposition to them would appear to be a form of hostility to sexual pleasure pursued for its own sake rather than for the sake of reproduction. The ban on sex toys is in that sense very closely linked to the older bans on contraceptives.

The district court followed the type of reasoning used in *Bowers*: they defined the putative right extremely narrowly, as the "right to publicly promote obscene devices," and then they concluded that the Fourteenth Amendment did not protect such a right. The court of appeals, following *Lawrence*, saw the issue as one of sexual liberty more generally: the right "to engage in private intimate conduct free from government intrusion." They argue that *Lawrence* protects this right in very general terms.

What of the fact that it was only "promotion," not use, that the statute criminalized? The court notes that "promotion" was a key issue in both *Griswold* (where the plaintiffs were contraceptive counselors) and *Eisenstadt* (where the plaintiff was a distributor of contraceptives). Even if use itself is not criminal in this case, they argue, "bans on commercial transactions involving a product can unconstitutionally burden individual substantive due process rights."

In other words, they recognize that the protection of sexual liberty is a matter that may involve the protection of transactions in the "public" domain. The counterargument that the law reflects the "moral judgment of the Texas legislature" is rejected as insufficient, when a protected Fourteenth Amendment right is being burdened. Again, *Lawrence* is cited in support of the idea that such protected rights cannot be infringed merely because a majority does not like the practices in question.

Does the law restrict "the sale of sex"? The court grants for the sake of argument that the state may regulate prostitution and public sex. They conclude, however, that this case, involving "the sale of a device that an individual may choose to use during intimate conduct with a partner in the home" is not in the same category.

Slightly earlier, the Eleventh Circuit upheld a similar Alabama law. (Unlike the Texas law, the statute explicitly exempted "ribbed condoms, and virility drugs.") The court reasoned that *Lawrence* did not apply, because *Lawrence* protected only "*private* sexual conduct," whereas the Alabama law "forbids *public, commercial* activity." They classified the sale of sex toys as "the sale of sex," along with prostitution. The opinion appears to have confused sexual activity that is itself commercial (sex for money) with commercial transactions that assist personal intimate consensual and noncommercial sexual choices. (Such a confusion is encouraged by the ambiguity of the language of "private" and "public" in the whole line of cases leading to *Lawrence*.) Sex for money is not constitutionally protected under *Lawrence*, but the sale of dildos and vibrators is not sex for money. Commercial transactions that assist intimate personal choices seem difficult to distinguish from the protected acts of the contraceptive counselors in *Griswold*, a problem the court does not even notice.

The Texas holding, then, represents a far more convincing reading of *Lawrence*. It shows that *Lawrence*, carefully read, protects not only consensual conduct, but also related "promotion," some of which includes commercial transactions. The occasional use of the words "the home" in the opinion make for confusion, since it's obvious that the relevant issue is the fact that adults use these products consensually and in seclusion, not that they use them in a special place. However, on the whole the opinion protects adult sexual choices from government intrusion, even when those choices require the purchase of unpopular products. Some day the conflict between the circuits may be resolved by the Supreme Court, but it is also possible that the few states with such laws will abandon them sooner.

One obstacle to the holding, though not one discussed by the Texas court, is *Stanley v. Georgia*, in which the use of pornography was held to be protected, on First Amendment free speech grounds, only insofar as that use was confined to the home. Under *Stanley*, the sale of obscenity could still be criminalized. It would appear that if the commercial sale of a vibrator is constitutionally protected, then the commercial sale of obscenity should also be protected—if not on First Amendment grounds, then on due process grounds. So the Texas holding awaits further clarification, along with the confusion over privacy that, as we argued, *Stanley* represents.

Does the Texas holding suggest that *Lawrence* might be used to defend sexual activity in sex clubs? If we forget about those unfortunate references to "the home," it does suggest an extension of *Lawrence* in that direction. Having laid down the principle that even activities that have commercial aspects enjoy constitutional protection, if they are key to the protection of a due process liberty, a court could reasonably find that in the choice to go to a sex club and engage in specific consensual practices there is an aspect of the liberty protected in *Lawrence*, and that the closing of commercial establishments unconstitutionally burdens that right. As in *Reliable Consultants*, such a court could clearly distinguish the provision of a support structure for chosen sexual practices from the "sale of sex."

If such a case were to come forward, the state or municipality in question would surely argue that not just "public morality" but also "public health" gave them a good reason to regulate sex businesses. Sex toys do not spread disease, they would argue, but sex clubs do. But that argument, as we have seen, is extremely flimsy. So if judges looked at the issue with a nonphobic eye, they could plausibly find that *Lawrence* protected the clubs. But this will not happen any time in the near future.

Finally, we arrive at an area in which the Supreme Court has grappled with the protection of adult establishments—but under the Free Speech Clause of the First Amendment rather than under the Fourteenth Amendment. The intricacies of the interpretation of that clause are beyond the scope of this book, but one case is of interest because it exhibits the same flawed reasoning that we observed in the nuisance cases.

J. R.'s Kitty Kat Lounge is a bar in South Bend, Indiana, that provided striptease dancing, culminating in total nudity, for the entertainment of patrons. Glen Theatre, similarly, provided nude dancing, though without serving alcohol. The state of Indiana, however, passed an ordinance against "Public Indecency," banning nudity in "a public place" (a concept that the ordinance did not define). It defined nudity as "the showing of the human male or female genitals, pubic area, or buttocks with less than opaque covering, the showing of the female breast with less than a fully opaque covering of any part of the nipple, or the showing of the covered male genitals in a discernibly turgid state." Plaintiffs Darlene Miller, Gayle Sutro, and Carla Johnson were nude dancers. Indiana conceded that their dancing was not obscene.

When the case was heard by the Seventh Circuit Court of Appeals in Chicago, the court held that the dancing was protected expression and that the ordinance was therefore unconstitutional. The most significant opinion was the long concurrence by Judge Richard

Posner. Posner did something pretty rare for a judge: he actually looked into the history of the topic in a serious way, asking what nude dancing is about in the Western tradition of the dance, and what role the nudity plays in the dancing and the message it communicates. He argues that the dance is expressive: it contains a message having to do with the value of eroticism. "[W]hether one has a taste or a distaste for erotic dance in general or striptease dances in particular, to say as the district judge did in this case that a striptease dance is not 'expressive activity,' but 'mere conduct,' is indefensible and a threat to artistic freedom." In communicating the message of eroticism, the nudity of the dancers plays an important role. Dancers garbed in G–string and pasties, as the ordinance required, would not be able to communicate exactly the same message.

Posner also points out that nude dancing is widely tolerated if it is part of "high art"—he cites a performance of Richard Strauss's *Salome* in which the Dance of the Seven Veils ended, as Strauss wished, in actual nudity. But, he continues, an elite prejudice against popular culture allows more interference with nude performance when the dancers are at the Kitty Kat Lounge: "The First Amendment forbids this kind of discrimination."

When the case was appealed to the Supreme Court, the Seventh Circuit was overruled by a 5–4 vote. Three different opinions were written on the majority side. All concurred that the nude dancing was expressive activity. Chief Justice Rehnquist, Justice O'Connor, and Justice Kennedy held that incidental limitations on First Amendment freedoms can be justified by an "important or substantial governmental interest." The "incidental effects" doctrine protects laws that are not directed at speech, but have an impact on speech. For example, a law forbidding open fires in public places can constitutionally be applied to a person who burns an American flag on a public street, because the law is not directed at speech and has only an incidental effect. In this case, in the view of the plurality, an interest in "protecting social order and morality," "unrelated to the suppression of free expression," justifies the incidental burdens on the dancers' expressive activity.

Justice White, dissenting, argues that a law that bans nudity only in some contexts (not, for example, in the home), and that burdens a significant amount of expressive activity needs to be scrutinized more rigorously, at a higher level of review, to see what the state's purpose is. Laws against public nudity, he contends, are designed to protect nonconsenting parties from offense:

> But that could not possibly be the purpose of preventing nude dancing in theaters and barrooms, since the viewers are exclusively consenting adults who pay money to see these dances. The purpose of the proscription in these contexts is to protect the viewers from what the State believes is the harmful message that nude dancing communicates.

In other words, *in these contexts* the state's purpose is not in fact unrelated to the suppression of expressive activity. This opinion captures neatly the distinctions that our argument has sought to draw throughout.

For Justice Scalia, replying to Justice White, the dancing is expressive, but the general law regulating public nudity is not specifically directed against expression, and this means that it is "not subject to normal First Amendment scrutiny." In his view, then, the government need show only a rational basis for the law, which it can easily do: "moral opposition to nudity" supplies that basis.

Both the plurality opinion and Scalia's concurrence are Devlinesque, Neither is interested in any tangible harms to the nonconsenting; both conclude that moral condemnation of what is going on behind closed doors is sufficient to carry the day. Justice

White, by contrast, is a Millian, focused on the question of consent and imposition. The two Devlinesque opinions, however, do not define the law as it currently exists, because it is the narrowest opinion that controls, and the narrowest opinion (in the sense of offering the least sweeping justification for a burden on expressive activity) is Justice Souter's concurrence. It is this opinion that intersects in fascinating ways with the public nuisance debate.

Souter begins by stating that while a dance performance is expressive activity, nudity is not, because it is "a condition, not an activity, and the voluntary assumption of that condition, without more, apparently expresses nothing beyond the view that the condition is somehow appropriate to the circumstances." Out the window is Posner's comprehensive history of nudity in the dance. Out the window too (unmentioned, unrebutted) is Posner's contention that the nudity in striptease dancing is an essential element of the message of eroticism communicated by the dancing.

Souter agrees with the plurality that government must show a legitimate interest to justify incidental burdens on expressive activity. (He implicitly refuses White's contention that the interest must be compelling.) He disagrees, however, about the nature of that interest. Without rejecting the plurality's Devlinesque justification, he puts forward a different rationale, one that focuses on actual and potential harms. According to Souter, the most pertinent government interest that might be cited to defend the ban on nudity in adult entertainment performances is one in "preventing prostitution, sexual assault, and other criminal activity." He calls these "harmful secondary effects." How should we understand this reasoning?

The claim that nude dancing leads to crimes against nonconsenting parties—sexual assault, and perhaps theft and other forms of criminal activity is a Millian claim, and it would seem that Souter is arguing that nude dancing harms nonconsenting parties. His language is unsatisfying: the term "criminal activity" is extremely vague, and the example of prostitution, a victimless crime, does not reassure us that the argument is indeed Millian. But let's suppose it is. We still have questions to pose. First, on what evidence does Souter base his claim? And remember the claim purportedly distinguishes dancing with pasties and a G-string from dancing in the nude. Souter says that he does not need concrete evidence. Instead, he notes that several cities assert that crime is correlated with the presence of "adult" entertainments. But this is hardly proof.

We also need to ask how tight the causal connection between performance and crime must be, in order to justify restrictions on expression. And how large a difference must exist between pastie performance and nude performance? Finally, what evidence justifies the conclusion that nudity causes the problem, as distinguished from other elements of a "lounge" that might be linked to crime, such as its location in a bad neighborhood and the availability of alcohol?

Justice Souter's opinion does not treat these issues seriously. What Souter is attempting to do is to cast the nude element in the dance as a nuisance in the Millian sense, but the extremely casual way in which he does this is disconcerting. Even if he is not attempting to show a compelling governmental interest in the regulation, he should not have been satisfied by these flimsy contentions.

Moreover, isn't there a narrower or less burdensome way to curb the illegal activity, namely to crack down on illegal activity while allowing the dancers to perform in the nude? This question, mentioned in the dissent, and central to the public nuisance cases, is nowhere addressed in Justice Souter's opinion.

The conclusion that the mere absence of pasties on the nipples of dancers causes sexual assault is a very odd, even absurd, conclusion. A long tradition of thinking of sex businesses as sources of disease and corruption lies in the background of his opinion, explaining the fact that he feels no need to provide solid empirical evidence for his conclusions.

Nude dancing continues to generate complex First Amendment questions.[14] What is important for our purposes is that the idea of diffuse public harms in connection with sex-related businesses has extraordinary tenacity, generating restrictions that cannot be justified by solid evidence. A priori reasoning of this sort is a tip-off that we are really not dealing with a Millian politics of harm, but with a form of Devlin's politics of disgust.

The bad reasoning exhibited in the public nuisance area does offer a number of hooks for constitutional argument. The free speech area is too narrow to do much work protecting clubs of this sort, since at most it is only the expressive activities of performers that enjoy protection. The equal protection avenue has not yet been pursued. Most promising is the extension of the *Lawrence* idea of intimate liberty to areas outside the home. Such an extension will not take place, however, without clarification of our murky legal notions of the public and the private.

5. PUBLIC AND PRIVATE: CONFUSION AND MORE CONFUSION

In *832 Corporation, Inc., 225 Corporation, Inc., and the John Adams Club, Inc. v. Gloucester Township*,[15] the U.S. District Court for the District of New Jersey upheld a very burdensome zoning and licensing requirement for "adult use" establishments in a way that focused attention on the commercial, hence "public," character of the businesses. The plaintiffs urged that *Lawrence* protected consensual adult sexual activity within such an establishment (secluded from the gaze of those who do not voluntarily enter the premises). The District Court rejects this reading of *Lawrence*, emphasizing those portions of the opinion that make reference to the home.

They wave away Justice Kennedy's other statements, saying: "Although *Lawrence* rejected the idea that such liberty was specifically placed within the home, it emphasized the private nature of the conduct"—and then, in a breathtakingly question-begging move, they interpret "private" to mean "in private settings," by which they mean: in some homelike place, and certainly not in a commercial establishment. They then go on to show that the clubs in question could not be exempted as private clubs because their membership and admissions procedures were not highly selective (they advertised on the internet), and thus they fall under the generally used definition of a "public accommodation."

As the sex toy cases already show us, the ambiguities of *Lawrence* cause confusion. Similarly, in a case involving a New York S and M club (involving the conditions under which a landlord may evict a tenant), the plaintiffs (Evening of the Unusual, Inc.) contend that consensual sexual conduct, not harmful to others and not involving either disorder or prostitution, is protected behavior that may not be used as a basis for eviction.[16] The Civil Court of the City of New York, New York County, finds that the behavior in question is not "private," ergo not protected, because it occurs in a "commercial establishment."[17]

The law contains not one public/private distinction, but several. We have already encountered:

1. A distinction between conduct that belongs to a protected sphere of personal decision making and other areas of conduct: *Lawrence* uses the name "private" for the former.
2. A distinction between conduct that occurs in a protected place ("the home"? other places relevantly like it?) and non-protected places. (*Stanley* makes this relevant to the legality of using pornography; *Lawrence* suggests, unclearly, that it may be relevant to the protection of intimate sexual conduct.)

[193]

In discussing the problems with using the home as a paradigm of the "private," we introduced a further distinction, which is implicit at least in many legal situations:

3. A distinction between conduct that is self-regarding, affecting the interests and rights of consenting parties only, and conduct that is, in Mill's sense, other-regarding, affecting the interests of people who do not consent.

And we argued that this distinction, while not very closely associated with distinction 2, is closely associated with a further distinction:

4. A distinction between conduct that is secluded from nonconsenting parties and conduct that is not secluded, but impinges on the interests of nonconsenting parties. (The former is "private," the latter "public.")

The legal distinction between "private nuisance" and "public nuisance" suggests a fifth idea:

5. A distinction between an event that affects the rights of one individual (who may then sue for damages or abatement) and an event that affects the rights of members of the community more widely, in such a way that it makes little sense to give each affected individual a damage action, and more sense to entrust government with the job of controlling the nuisance.

This distinction is not the same as either (3) or (4), since a private nuisance often does not involve any seclusion and is defined by the idea of a harm; the conduct in question has to be other-regarding in Mill's sense, and is thus not secluded in the sense relevant to (4). Public nuisances, we said, are almost always other-regarding as well, involving harm to people who do not consent.

Finally, we must now introduce a sixth distinction:

6. A distinction between a "public accommodation" and a private facility. Public accommodations typically include hotels, inns, restaurants, movie houses, retail stores, transportation facilities, museums, libraries, schools, gyms, and many more such establishments. On the other side would be private clubs of various sorts.

It's important to see that this last distinction is different from all the others. A "private" accommodation needn't involve protected intimate activities: usually the distinction between the two types of facilities is made by looking at the selectivity of membership criteria, rather than the types of activities involved. A "public" facility, on the other side, may involve intimate conduct: sex businesses large enough and unselective enough to be denominated "public" are paradigms. As for the third distinction, a private facility usually involves only consenting adult parties, though not always. (Children are present in a private country club, for example.) But it certainly isn't true that a facility that is a public accommodation in the legal sense always includes people who have not consented to witness the acts that go on there. Once again, sex businesses and bathhouses are handy examples of businesses that cater only to those who choose to witness or engage in certain acts. Moreover, though "public" in the sense of counting (often, at least) as "public accommodations," they may be, and usually are, secluded from the view of prying eyes.

What is the point of the distinction between a public accommodation and a private facility? One central role for such a distinction is to draw lines around the reach of antidiscrimination laws. Typically, a private facility, such as a small members-only club, will be protected against charges that it has violated antidiscrimination laws in areas such as disability, sexual orientation, and so forth. A public accommodation will have to conform to those rules. There is thus a rationale for making the definition of public accommodation very broad: a decent society wants to protect its members from discrimination of these kinds even when they are in places where only consenting adults go. Thus it's good that any business of a certain size contain ramps for wheelchairs, whether or not it involves activity that has an impact on nonconsenting parties.

It should be obvious that the fact that something is a public accommodation for the purposes of antidiscrimination law has nothing to do with the rationale for regulating (and not regulating) sexual conduct, which typically (when it is reasonable) derives from our third and fourth distinctions. Many sex businesses do not have taxing membership selection processes; but they do require a fee, and in that way, and often in further ways as well (registration, application), they guarantee that the acts performed within are self-regarding in Mill's sense. Again and again, however, courts have used the fact that a business is in technical terms a public accommodation to justify cracking down on the consensual activity that takes place there.

An early landmark in this regard is *Paris Adult Theatre I v. Slaton* (1973),[18] a case concerning the showing of two allegedly obscene films in a commercial theater to consenting adult audiences (where reasonable precautions had been taken to exclude minors). The Court leaned heavily on *Stanley v. Georgia*, where the equation of "private" with the home had set up a privileged zone for viewing such materials, associating privacy with our second distinction. They argued that no commercial establishment, however careful to exclude the nonconsenting, could count as "private" in the relevant sense. "[T]he idea of a 'privacy' right and a place of public accommodation are, in this context, mutually exclusive," wrote the majority. This case has subsequently been used, in turn, to support various punitive policies directed at adult establishments. The closing of the bathhouses in New York City in 1986 was defended with appeal to the distinction between a "private home" and "commercial establishments," invoking *Paris Adult Theatre I.*

The confusions of the *Griswold-Lawrence* sequence of privacy cases have long tentacles, reaching out to a diverse range of cases and choking off serious thought regarding the sort of conduct we should agree to protect.

6. A RATIONAL POLICY: SECLUSION AND THE SELF-REGARDING

What would a rational public policy look like in this area? Let's focus on constitutional issues, as far as they take us. First of all, where erotic performance is concerned, we should see the wisdom in Judge Posner's analysis and conclude that nudity is an expressive element in certain sorts of dance performances and is therefore protected by the First Amendment. A ban on public nudity is therefore unconstitutional unless it includes exceptions for expressive activity.

Outside the performance context, an attractive approach would be to adopt the Millian distinction between self-regarding and other-regarding conduct as the relevant one for the protection of intimate sexual conduct and accompanying nudity (distinction 3), and to grant that seclusion (distinction 4) is often a good proxy for the self-regarding. The so-called privacy right should be interpreted in light of these two distinctions. In other words, *Lawrence* would be read broadly, as the plaintiffs in *832 Corporation* wish, to protect consensual secluded adult conduct, even when it occurs in an establishment that is commercial, hence a "public accommodation" for the purposes of discrimination law. If crimes (sexual assault, theft, prostitution—though I believe that the last should not be a crime) take place in such an establishment, the police should enforce the law. They should not, however, penalize the establishment, whether by burdensome regulation or by an uncompensated "taking."

Zoning may be used to distinguish residential from commercial areas, but its use to squeeze sex businesses into economically marginal or dangerous areas of conduct is probably unconstitutional (under the expansive reading of the privacy right that I'm adopting). Just as in *Cleburne* where a zoning regulation that fenced out a home for people with mental retardation was held to lack a rational basis and to be grounded in mere animus (see chapter 2), so too here: attempts to zone out adult bookstores and other related establishments should probably be held to lack a rational basis—unless an argument can be made that is better than any we've heard so far.

Worries about the spread of disease, insofar as they are rational, can be handled by a requirement that all adult establishments prominently post warnings concerning HIV and other STDs, and that they supply condoms to all who wish to use them. Beyond that, however, the decision to take a health risk in sexual activity should be treated as like any other decision to risk one's health, by overeating, or smoking, or climbing mountains: one's own to make, criminal only when it violates the rights of another. (Los Angeles requires that bathhouses get county health licenses costing $1000 per year, allow quarterly health inspections, and provide on-site HIV testing. They also request that signs, condoms, and adequate lighting be available to discourage high-risk sex. Such rules seem about as far as the law is entitled to go, and some of them—the expensive license, the expensive on-site HIV testing—may go too far.)

We've been dealing with clubs that fence out the nonconsenting by an admissions policy. What about sex in public restrooms, or in the woods, or parks—places that often are secluded but involve a risk of imposition on the nonconsenting? Such places are often important for sexual activity among gay men, and criminalizing all sex in such locations often leads to inquisitorial police behavior, including entrapment, so for the Millian it would be good to look skeptically on that diminution of people's space for consensual activity, while at the same time protecting the public, and especially children, from direct offense.

One reasonable policy was adopted by the Massachusetts State Police. In 2001, a policy directive instructed police officers not to take action aimed at preventing people from meeting for sex at roadside rest stops. If the activity is adequately hidden from public view, the police are not to interfere: the test is whether there is "substantial risk" that the conduct will be observed by a casual passerby. The most important aspect of the policy is that officers may not ask someone to leave an area simply because they think that the person has the intent to have sexual activity. (Often people use the area to meet people for later sex in a more secluded place.)

The city of Amsterdam, in the Netherlands, has recently permitted sex in the Vondelpark, and it appears that the same policy will shortly be extended to all public parks in the nation. The policy statement notes that most such behavior is secluded and does not cause "any actual nuisance"; if there is offensive behavior that is visible from the public path, that behavior would not be protected under the new rule. Moreover, condoms must always be cleared away, no sexual activity may take place in the neighborhood of children's playgrounds, and the permission covers only evening and nighttime hours. One reason explicitly mentioned for the change in policy is that regulating sex in the park, rather than targeting it, helps the whole community to protect gay people from "queer-bashers," who now often prey on gays wherever they believe that gays will be unwilling or unable to call the police to their aid.

Disgust, as we have seen it throughout this book, is an unreliable force that masks many forms of stigma and hierarchy. I have argued that disgust can be a good basis for lawmaking when its operation is harmlike, following the guidelines laid down in the traditional law of nuisance. In another group of cases, where there is direct sensory contact but no clear physical damage (public masturbation, sex before the unwilling eyes of others), the community may be entitled to restrict the conduct under law, because the element of unwilling imposition brings the offense in question close to the first group of cases. In still other cases, disgust may be a route to a legal restriction that is best defended on grounds of harm to nonconsenting others: thus, laws against eating dog meat, or laws against sex with animals are good laws because they protect animals, and disgust gets the right result without having to convert obtuse people who do not care about animal cruelty. We should beware, however, of relying on disgust in such cases since the fact that disgust reaches a right result in these cases may strengthen our disposition to rely on it in other cases where it does not track harm to others.

Finally, there is the very large group of cases in which there is no sensory confrontation at all, but only what Mill called a "purely constructive" injury, occasioned by thinking about what is going on behind someone else's closed doors. I have argued that such cases are never rightly regulated by law, and certainly not when what is at stake is a fundamental right of intimate personal choice that we have already decided to protect on Fourteenth Amendment due process grounds. This chapter has argued that, despite appearances, many cases of "public" sex fall in this category—wherever there is no unwilling imposition on nonconsenting parties—and that the sexual choices involved should probably be seen as constitutionally protected.

The United States is not a Millian nation. Ideas of public morality still control a good deal of our legal thinking in the area of public nudity and public sex. I suggest, however, that we will be a lot better off if we at least understand how much of our legacy of distaste for sex businesses is motivated by obscure ideas of nonmarital sex as contaminating, a disease seeping out into the community. The politics of disgust has prevented us from thinking clearly and coming up with good reasons for what we may or may not want to regulate. Another reason why thought has been so sloppy in this area is the messy concept of privacy and its limits, and I think we would all be a great deal better off if we observed the distinctions outlined here and did not slide irrationally from one understanding of "private" to the other.

If we clear away all those confusions, we might be left with some weighty non-Millian reasons in favor of the regulation of sex businesses—or, what I suspect is far more likely—we would see that all the non-Millian reasons are outgrowths of the politics of disgust, and we would appreciate the wisdom of the limits that Mill proposed.

1. Even this type may raise questions about constitutional rights, if a basic right is involved and the harm is not grave.

2. Thus, although Blackstone recognizes a nuisance that he calls "incorporeal," his example is someone blocking a path that leads to your land, or "putting logs across it, or ploughing over it" (III.13.2).

3. For a typical example, see *Baltimore v. Warren Mfg.*, 59 Md. 96 (1882), where either danger or the property of being "offensive to taste or smell" is sufficient.

4. *Commonwealth v. Perry*, 139 Mass. 198 (1885). The state argues that "said odors produced discomfort, sickness, and disgust to some of the occupants of said dwelling-houses; that at times they were so intense that some of said occupants were obliged to close their doors and windows; that said odors were the odors natural to swine, described by one witness as 'pig odors,' and by another as 'the odor of one pig multiplied five hundred times,' and by one other as 'the odor of a piggery.' It was conceded that no swill, slops, or unclean food were fed to said swine, but that they were fed only on good grains, beets, and other vegetables."

5. *Kriener v. Turkey Valley Community School Dist.*, 212 N. Y. 2d 526 (Iowa 1973). A witness testified that she could not eat when the wind was blowing

from the lagoon toward her home: "Well, I know I went home for dinner different times, and I couldn't eat. If I would start frying meat or something, why, it would just about bring my breakfast up, and rather than that I would just quit and forget eating."

6. Horace Gay Wood, *A Practical Treatise on the Law of Nuisances in Their Various Forms; Including Remedies Therefore at Law and in Equity* (Albany, N.Y.: John B. Parsons, Jr., 1875).

7. Cited, *inter alia*, in *Trevett v. Prison Ass'n of Virginia*, 98 Va. 332 (1900), another water-rights case. Note that this text, and some of the cases, permit legal action when the disgusting substance does not yet impinge on the senses. But this exception does not appear to admit a "purely constructive" injury of the sort we have found problematic in chapter 3: the theory of the cases is that the substance would, present over time in sufficient quantities, occasion danger or sensory disgust, or both. See Martha Nussbaum, *Hiding from Humanity:Disgust, Shame, and the Law* (Princeton: Princeton University Press, 2004), 160–61.

8. The point of recognizing a distinct category here is that with private nuisance the person affected has a right of action; but it seems impractical to give every member of the public a right of action in case of a more general nuisance, so that sort of case is dealt with differently, by public regulation. Some of the descriptions of the category (e.g., in Blackstone) involve a few apparently non-Millian items in the category of public nuisance, such as gambling houses, houses of prostitution, and inns that turn away travelers without good reason. It seems, however, that Blackstone actually thinks these establishments cause some type of public harm, although he does not articulate that theory.

9. *Black's Law Dictionary*, quoted in *Mutschler v. Phoenix* 212 Ariz. 160, 129P.3d 71 (App. 2006).

10. *Mutschler* at 163 n. 6, 166 (citations omitted).

11. For this subtext in the play, see the relevant chapter in Jonathan Dollimore and Alan Sinfield, *Political Shakespeare: Essays in Cultural Materialism* (Ithaca, NY: Cornell University Press, 1994).

12. The cases find no unwilling imposition: see for example *31 W. 21st St v. Evening of the Unusual* (N.Y. Civ. Ct. 1984). "Ms. Sullivan [an undercover journalist] testified that she did not participate in any of the activities and, with the exception of one incident, she was not propositioned or confronted by any of the patrons. This one confrontation occurred when she was approached by a man who told her he wanted to be 'disciplined' and offered her $100 if she would perform certain explicit sadomasochistic sexual acts upon him. She declined his generous offer."

13. *Reliable Consultants v. Earle*, 517 F. 3d 738 (5th Cir. 2008); *Williams v. Alabama*, 511 U.S. 1012 (2004).

14. See for example *Schultz v. Cumberland*, 26 F. Supp. 1126, 1144 (W. D. Wis. 1998), arguing that some excessively burdensome restrictions on an adult business were unconstitutional on First Amendment grounds.

15. 404 F. Supp. 2d. 614 (D.N.J. 2005).

16. *31 W. 21st St. Associates v. Evening of the Unusual, Inc.*, 125 Misc. 2d 661; 480 N.Y.S. 2d 816; 1984 N.Y. Misc. LEXIS 3466.

17. *City of New York v. St. Mark's Baths*. 497 N.Y.S. 2d 979, 983.

18. 413 U.S. 49 (1973).

After Disgust?

I am he who tauntingly compels men, women, nations, Crying,
Leap from your seats and contend for your lives!

—WALT WHITMAN,
BY BLUE ONTARIO'S SHORE

My name is Harvey Milk, and I'm here to recruit you.

THE LATE HARVEY MILK, POLITICIAN AND ACTIVIST

It would be nice to think that the United States today is no longer a
nation in which disgust at another group of human beings is widespread. In race relations, we have made amazing and wonderful
strides from the politics of disgust to the politics of humanity. I was
brought up by a father (from the deep South)—a highly educated
man, a partner in a large Philadelphia law firm—who seriously

believed that it was unclean and contaminating for a white person to drink from a glass that had previously been used by a black person, or to use a toilet that had been used by a black person. Those ideas of contamination and taint, which once were enacted in law—in the Jim Crow regime of separate drinking fountains, swimming pools, lunch counters—really do appear to have faded. No doubt some people who voted for President Obama did so while holding such views, simply because they thought him the better choice on policy. No doubt some who voted against him opposed him for such reasons. But such attitudes are increasingly rare, and in the next generation, small children who grow up modeling themselves on Sasha and Malia Obama will be likely to lack them altogether. In this area, law took the lead, defending the equal rights of African-Americans long before Americans had come to a consensus about racial matters. Over time, the associational rights guaranteed under law changed the ways in which people lived together.

A similar transformation is slowly taking place in the area of sexual orientation, but the process is still incomplete. Many Americans still do shrink from gays and lesbians and consider themselves somehow defiled by them. But the ideas of contamination and defilement are under siege from the forces of imagination and humanity. In this area, unlike the area of race, the law has been relatively slow to protect equal rights, and the impetus toward a politics of humanity has come, more often, from the friendships of young people and, perhaps above all, from the arts, which have given us models of dignity, equality, and joy that can hardly fail to work upon people's insides in ways that prompt change. Ralph Ellison called his novel *Invisible Man* "a raft of perception, hope, and entertainment" on which America might negotiate the "snags and whirlpools" that stand between us and our democratic ideals.[1] What he meant, I think, was that these three qualities all must go together. Entertainment makes perception possible: pleasure makes people willing to receive another person's shape into their minds and hearts. That shape of a body with skin of a different color slips into the mind so pleasingly that one never stops to think in terms of defilement. And this possibility of empathy, in turn, prompts hope. The arts have given us many powerful images of gay and lesbian lives, and we have all, straight and gay, been changed by those images.

Especially powerful recently was the critical and popular success of *Milk*, Gus Van Sant's film based on the life of California politician Harvey Milk. Here we could see audiences of all backgrounds and ages rooting for a gay hero—and not, as in the case of *Brokeback Mountain*, for heroes who were despairing and trapped. Harvey Milk was a success. He was competent, widely respected, dynamic. He was also a joyous human being, whose infectious generosity and high spirits changed others. (That's why he was so threatening to the tormented man who later shot him.) Audiences of all sorts cheer him as he runs to become the first openly gay man elected to public office in California. They also follow with sympathy his attempts to find love and to balance love with political engagement. Audiences even inwardly cheer the highly subversive line with which Milk, mocking the politics of defilement and contagion, typically opened his speeches: "My name is Harvey Milk, and I'm here to recruit you." The idea of "recruitment," used by the politics of disgust to talk about contamination and cooptation into a filthy lifestyle, is here turned on its head: not, "I am here to sicken you and spread my contagion," but, "I am here to ask you to join a movement for freedom and inclusion." I am here to recruit you into the politics of humanity, the effort to secure equal dignity and the opportunity for the pursuit of happiness. The film, in turn, recruits the audience, and the response to its solicitation suggests that huge numbers of Americans want to be recruited just like that—into a fight for justice, into the demand for equality. I can tell you that once, not too long ago, a large proportion of the straight men of my acquaintance would have shrunk from that slogan with fear and a sense of defilement. That so many react both calmly and positively today shows us a lot about ourselves.

The film serves as a reminder of where the politics of sexual orientation has been and a harbinger of where it is going. It reminds its audience of the repression and stigmatization—and, of course, in its tragic climax, the violence—that used to confront gay men and lesbians, and often still does confront them. But it also reminds us of the distance American society has traveled from that time. Its audience witnesses an era before sodomy laws had been struck down, before nondiscrimination laws were widespread, before the issue of same-sex marriage was even on the table. The very location of our current controversies itself provides reason for optimism.

Even more hopeful, in a sense, is Sean Penn's astonishing portrayal of Harvey Milk, for which he won the Screen Actors' Guild Award and an Oscar. Straight male macho actors used to shun playing gay characters, and ideas of disgust and defilement were a major part of what drove them away. Even if they did not feel personally defiled by the exercise of letting that person into their hearts and heads and bodies (and, no doubt, many did), their audiences would surely feel that the image of that male star bore, from that point on, a conspicuous taint. Other male stars had broken the barrier, but rarely with the combination of overt sexuality and sheer happiness that Penn displayed, a happiness that was perhaps Milk's most radical and threatening aspect. A gay man could be nonthreatening if he were pure or demure; or if he were a failure, like one of Devlin's incompetent sex addicts; or if he were tormented and squashed, like the characters in *Brokeback Mountain*. But Milk, as Penn played him, was none of those things. His demand was not for pity (compatible with disgust), but for respect and shared enjoyment. He clearly enjoyed being himself and led a competent life focused on many diverse goals. And this image of the gay man is truly threatening to the politics of disgust. Penn, whose macho persona usually suggests some smoldering rage ready to explode, discovered inside himself capacities for sensuousness, playfulness, and exuberant joy, and gave what seems to me by far his sexiest performance. For a straight man to allow a gay man's mind and sexuality to enter himself is as decisive a rejection of the politics of disgust as can be imagined.

So the politics of humanity is making strides. And yet, in our pained struggles over same-sex marriage, disgust still plays a silent role. And in our attitudes toward bathhouses and "public" sex, we still see disgust on a rampage.

Much of the force behind the politics of humanity must come from broad social change. Where, in all this, is law? In race relations, I said, law took the lead, and social change followed. In the politics of sexual orientation, law—and certainly constitutional law—has led more cautiously, and has at times been a follower. But law has been a far from insignificant force. Constitutional law expresses our deepest sense, as a society, of what freedom and equality are; of what it means to have fundamental rights; of what it means to have certain protected areas of both liberty and equality that are seen as inherent in the very idea of human dignity. If entertainments such as *Will and Grace* and *Milk* change hearts, the resonant language, and the holdings, of *Lawrence* and *Romer* change the institutional structures in which we live our daily lives together, expressing an inclusive sense of respect for people and committing the nation to defending some zones of freedom and nondiscrimination for all.

Law needs to do a lot more work before the progress that is underway in this area will be anything like complete. The notion of privacy articulated in *Lawrence* and related cases is confused and confusing. Work needs to be done to separate its constituent notions and to establish protection for secluded consensual acts that take place outside the home. Nondiscrimination law is currently piecemeal and local: we need a federal nondiscrimination statute that will do for sexual orientation what Title VII did for gender. (And then there will be much more legal work to do interpreting that law and ensuring that its protections remain robust.) In the area of marriage, the best we can hope for currently is an experimental state-by-state approach, which may well, over time, lessen resistance in other states. Right away, however, the intrusive Defense of Marriage Act, which prevents any state from creating a robust form of same-sex marriage, equal in entitlements to opposite-sex marriage, should be repealed. Let us hope that President Obama will stand by his opposition to that hate-inspired law.

Walt Whitman didn't think very highly of law. "To hold men together by paper and seal or by compulsion is no account," he wrote. "That only holds men together which aggregates all in a living principle," and he went on to say that only poets, and not judges, could supply that "something."[2] Here, I believe, Whitman underestimated the social force of "paper and seal." For paper and seal—although they surely need to be implemented to become more than words on paper—still have great expressive and dignitary power. Typically, they also have great practical power. We should not think that legal change can effect social change all on its own. That did not happen with race, and it will not happen here. Law, however, can set out parameters that express equal respect, ruling certain odious arrangements off-limits and guaranteeing all citizens the equal protection of the laws that exist. In this way law protects the rights of the vulnerable and sends a signal to the whole society that liberty and equality are made for us all.

NOTES

1. Ralph Ellison, Invisible Man (New York: Random house, 1992), xxiv–xxv.

2. *By Blue Ontario's Shore*, 130–31.

Index

INDEX

Turing, Alan, 28n13
Turner v. Safley, 151, 153–55

Unenumerated rights, 70–72, 104
U.S. v. Reidel, 92n24
U.S. v. Virginia, 42–43, 49
University of Chicago Press, 179

Varnum v. Brien, 166n26
Violence against gays and lesbians, 67–68, 96, 150
Virginia Military Institute, 42
Vondelpark, 199

Weininger, Otto, 18, 23, 29n25
West Virginia Board of Education v. Barnette, 93n35

White, Justice Byron, 79–80, 189
Whitman, Walt, 204, 209
Wilde, Oscar, 64–66, 82, 91n12, 116
Will and Grace, xvi, 208
Williams, Craig, 165n4
Williams, Roger, 37–39, 48
Williams v. Alabama, 203n13
Wisconsin v. Yoder, 83
Wolfenden Commission, xi, 9–10, 65
Wood, Gordon, 52n1, 52n7
Wood, Horace Gay, 173

Yoshino, Kenji, 93n30

Zablocki v. Redhail, 150–51, 153